The Little Book of Christian Character & Manners

The Little Book of Christian Character & Manners

WILLIAM & COLLEEN DEDRICK

HIBBARD
PUBLICATIONS

The Little Book of
Christian Character and Manners
by William and Colleen Dedrick

Published 2001 by Hibbard Publications
P.O. Box 3091
Wilmington, DE 19804

Cover & book design ©2001 by Mark Dinsmore,
  mark.dinsmore@verizon.net

ISBN 1-931343-14-4

Printed in the United States of America
06 05 04 03 02   6 5 4 3 2

To Gerald and Eileen Epp because their faithfulness to God's commands in bringing up their children is inspiring.

To the many families who encourage us by sharing how God has blessed their lives through the teaching of this book.

TABLE OF CONTENTS

Preface

*T*HE TEACHING OF THIS BOOK *is based on the presupposition that God's Word is the true final authority. God has given His people specific directions with regard to the rearing of children. To the extent that we rightly and consistently apply His instructions, His blessings will be bestowed upon us.*

We wish there were not a need to write this book, but such is not the case. Today's families are suffering because the concepts of Biblical family government—unknown to many in these last generations—have been replaced by humanistic and so-called "modern" ideas about child rearing that have produced anarchy in the home.

Home has become simply a "crash pad"—a place to make a quick stop for food, clothes, and sleep. Each family member's energies are focused on relationships and activities outside the home; there is little life within the family circle. The wisdom of past generations is disregarded;

hence, grandma and grandpa find it best to live far away. Fathers focus all their attention on their work outside the home to supply the material needs of the crash pad and the family's ever-increasing lust for entertainment. Mothers seek outside responsibilities in response to their discontent with life at home. Children put their trust in the wisdom of the group and seek security in peers, demanding more and more entertainment outside of the home.

But thanks to God a quiet reformation is taking place: the Biblical family is being revived, via home education, and will again strengthen our nation.

The return to a life centered around the home is possible only through a commitment to that life, a commitment that does not falter because of difficulty or hardship. Godly homes are built on conviction, commitment, and perseverance—qualities that are necessary to put into practice the principles in this book.

As you read, you may become aware of aspects of nurture you have neglected, areas in which you have failed in the training of your children. Your immediate reaction may be anger or a great sense of defeat. Our prayer is that you will instead be empowered by God's Spirit and Word to grow in the areas in which you have fallen short.

A word of caution is needed here concerning unloving behavior on the part of parents. Wickedness and immaturity in a parent's heart have no place in godly child training. Harshness should never be a substitute for strictness: the two are not synonymous. A loving strictness and the careful enforcing of rules is profitable for Christian discipline of children, but harshness— or a fit of anger that results in an attack on the body or character of the child—is a sin against God as well as the child. Harshness is a symptom of deep-rooted sin and can be remedied only through repentance, not group therapy and band-aid psychology.

Clearly this book is not meant to be a complete manual of infant care, a detailed instruction on etiquette, a comprehensive Bible study on family government, or an exhaustive list of all aspects of child training. Its purpose is to give parents a Biblical framework from which to view their calling as parents, and to provide enough actual examples to enable parents to apply Scripture to their own unique family situations.

It is expected that the Christian reader will be drawn to Scripture by the Spirit and that your every thought will be put in subjection to Christ. The Word commands the Christian parent to be "transformed by the renewing of your mind" (Romans 12:1,2), rather than to be conformed to the world's system of thinking. We trust that you will be challenged to follow the Lord completely in bringing up your children in His nurture and admonition.

Finally, to dispel any possible assumptions to the contrary, we are not perfect parents, nor do we have unusual or especially "good" children. We are sinners like all the rest of mankind and, because we are redeemed, we are still being sanctified. The Biblical concepts outlined herein are effectual when put into practice and, to the extent that we have obeyed God in these things, yes, we have reaped the blessing.

Mr. and Mrs. William Dedrick
April 13, 1992

Introduction

TODAY AN INCREASINGLY *common complaint is heard from young parents: they do not enjoy their own children!* The "me generation" has been forced to grow up—against its will—and this lack of enjoyment is one of the many consequences of the self-preoccupation that so characterizes that generation.

Children are seen as complications, or even obstacles, in the perpetual quest for fun, excitement, and fulfillment. To see this attitude among the ungodly is to be expected, since they have rejected God and His Word—the only source of abundant living. What should alarm us, however, is that Christians are making the same complaint.

In reality, these complaints by frazzled mothers worn out by "hyperactive" or "strong-willed" children (an earlier generation would have called them unruly) are merely symptoms of a disease. The root cause of this disease is the rejection of the commands of God: Christian families have brought this affliction upon themselves by following the "empty and deceitful" philosophies of the world.

Although most evangelicals pride themselves that they are—unlike the "liberal churches"—true to the Bible, many of these evangelical leaders and authors adhere to the same philosophy of child training as the non-Christian educators and psychologists. The secular philosophy asserts that today's children are different, that they need to be handled differently than children of Biblical times, or of the 1800s, or of the 1920s. A real test of which authority forms the basis for an author's arguments is to note how many "experts" (past or present) he feels compelled to quote. Often we are assured that the Bible agrees with Dr. Whozits, Psychologist So-and-So, Professor Whoever, or a particular scientific study; however, it is only the Word of God that is to give us the never-failing foundation and appropriate instruction for training our children.

Secular psychology and educational philosophy are based on false presuppositions and therefore are bankrupt. Secularists deny that man is an image-bearer of his great Creator, asserting that he is an evolving, higher animal that arrived here by chance. They also deny that man's problems are due to sin—a result of the Fall. Secular humanists insist instead that man's problems are outside himself, that they are the fault of his environment. In other words, in secular educational psychology and philosophy there is no God and man has been redefined. It is clear that these presuppositions, whether used by the Christian or non-Christian, can only guarantee the ultimate destruction of the family—parents as well as children.

If you truly want God's blessing on your home, we challenge you to get back to the Bible, the only true Word on the family. In the Bible you will find the true view of God and man. Deuteronomy 32:46,47 states, "Set your hearts on all the words . . . which you shall command your children to be careful to observe all the words of this law. For it is not a futile thing for you, because it is your life . . ." For a man to be blessed, he must see himself and his family from God's perspective. It is time for reformation and a return to Christian doctrine. We must again embrace the doctrines of historic Christianity, which accepted the Bible's view of man made in the image of God, fallen in all his being, and in need of redemption and sanctification.

Chapter 1

The Biblical Basis of Discipline

WHEN PARENTS ARE FRUSTRATED *about a specific problem they are having with a child, they will often discuss it with friends or question a respected person, seeking a solution for the difficulty they are experiencing. Particularly when parents believe the Bible is silent on a subject or does not give enough details, they rush after this book and that seminar searching for information that will tell them what to do in every possible case or situation. Many of these frustrating problems or difficult situations could be resolved with the Godly wisdom that comes from a basic understanding of what the Word teaches about child training.*

Therefore, it is essential that, first, you know what the Bible authoritatively says about bringing up children. Make this the very foundation of your thinking and you will have God-given confidence in rearing your children.

Crucial to the fulfilling of your responsibility as parents is understanding your position of authority. God has commanded fathers to have authority over their children. (See Genesis 18:19; Exodus 20:12; Leviticus 19:3,32; Deuteronomy 32:46,47; Deuteronomy 6:1–9; Hebrews 12:5–9; Ephesians 6:4; 1 Timothy 3:4,12.) Ignorance of, or willful disobedience of, this command is one of the greatest causes of uncertainty in training children. You have a God-given right to govern your child and to expect his obedience to your rule. You are not your child's "pal," nor should it be your goal to pursue that kind of relationship with him. When you understand and accept your position of authority and actively bring up your child with Godly nurture and admonition, you do reap the blessing of a joyful and close relationship with your child. Secular psychologists claim that their methods of child training guarantee a loving, trusting relationship between parent and child. Their claim is a false one, because it is not based on God's order. On the contrary, humanistic child training destroys the family as God intends it to be.

Parental authority is not to be carried out in an arbitrary or capricious manner, however. Encompassed in the concept of the God-ordained authority of parents is the responsibility to discipline their children. (See Ephesians 6:4; Deuteronomy 6:1–9.) The term "discipline," as used in this book, includes all of the training of the child—the chastening as well as the teaching. In other words, discipline is the order or control imposed upon the child's life and the instruction given to him by those responsible for his training.

Both the Deuteronomy and Ephesians passages make it clear that the Lord's way of discipline is two-pronged. First, there is to be training of character, or "nurture." God expects you to give your children training and instruction that will promote growth and maturity. The word "nurture" in Ephesians 6:4 is a translation of the Greek word "paideia," which means discipline that regulates character. It includes both chastening and teaching, and is a term for training by discipline. Popular psychology encourages us to see our children as developing through stages, each stage a little more unbearable than the previous one. The Christian parent must reject this thinking and nurture his child—encouraging his growth into a mature Christian. This was once the understood goal of child training. Note, for example, the entry in Webster's Dictionary of 1828, which states that nurture is "that which promotes growth; education; instruction; Ephesians 6."

The second prong of Biblical discipline is "admonition," or counsel to the understanding or intellect. In the Ephesians passage, admonition is the translation of the Greek word "nouthesia," which means words of encouragement or rebuke and warning. Through admonition we call the child's attention to what is right or wrong. The definition given for admonition in Webster's Dictionary of 1828 is "gentle reproof; counseling against a fault; instruction in duties; caution; direction." Admonition, then, is the verbal instruction and reproof that causes the mind to grow in discernment. Sadly, parents of today are sternly cautioned against damaging their child's self-esteem; correcting a fault is seen as negative and destructive of his fragile psyche. This is blatantly anti-Scriptural and has created weak, doting, confused parents and self-willed, self-centered children who do not respond to any instruction, words of caution, or direction from others.

Hand in hand with the honor of parental authority, then, comes the responsibility to chasten and teach your child. The parent who neglects or refuses to discipline his child is himself undisciplined and disobedient to God. The result of this neglect or refusal is an undisciplined child who comes to despise and reject all authority. This is perhaps another aspect of what the Apostle Paul meant in Ephesians 6:4 and

Colossians 3:21 when he warned fathers not to "provoke their children to wrath:" the Greek words mean "to exasperate and to cause a long-lasting anger"—anger that is the result of a lack of training or inconsistent and unreasonable discipline. If you question whether you are acting with Godly authority in your home, turn to Appendix A and give the list of warning signs prayerful consideration.

The consequences of rejecting God's order and authority for the family are grave; we have already begun to see the resulting breakdown of society. Parents who are unable to command obedience, whether through ignorance or willful disobedience, teach anarchy to the young. This has been true at previous times in history: the prophet Isaiah spoke of children in his day as oppressive, insolent rulers (Isaiah 3:4,5,12).

In this nation, the youth rebellion of the 1960s was a logical result of impotent leadership in homes that had been immersed in the teachings of Dr. Benjamin Spock in the 1940s and 1950s. God-ordained parental authority was replaced with the child's autonomous will, resulting in defiance and disregard of all authority. How very different are the results for a nation that honors the following command: "Correct your son, and he will give you rest; yes, he will give delight to your soul" (Proverbs 29:17).

There are three ways in which parents show their willful disregard for, or ignorance of, God's command to discipline children: lack of restraint—or failure to set standards—permissiveness, and neglect. Lack of restraint, the failure to set boundaries or standards and to give order to the child's life, is a common weakness among parents. In 1 Kings 1:5,6, the sad story is told of King David, in which he—a mighty warrior, a killer of giants, and a king—fails to set down the law for a son. This is a frequent sin of leaders as well as common men. Parents can neither afford to be oblivious to their child's actions nor fail to give direction to his activities.

Permissiveness is another common failure of parents. Permissiveness is the failure to chastise disobedient children, and shows dishonor to God. This problem is the focus of the story of Eli and his sons in 1 Samuel 2:22–32 and 3:13, in which we learn that chastening or discipline is much more than the mild reprimand Eli gave his sons. God let Eli know that his failure to discipline his sons for their disobedience was dishonoring to Him, and it resulted in His judgment on that family forever (2:29–32; 3:13,14).

The battle against permissiveness is a daily one for parents. Their own emotional weakness or leniency may prevent parents from taking proper action against disobedience, for example,

"You did not mean to hit Susie, did you?" In other cases, so many exceptions are made that the exceptions become the rule, for example, "I am going to count to . . ." In other instances, parents may find it difficult to see what is so bad that warrants chastening, that is, the behavior seems cute or normal. Parents need to realign themselves daily with God's standard of right and wrong and to honor God by upholding the right.

Finally, neglect can be a problem, even in families of believers. Parents may pride themselves that their children are nicely dressed, comfortably housed, and well-fed, and yet be neglectful in other ways. There are children who lack instruction and training because of their parents' misplaced values, such as career or work priorities, or self-fulfilling activities that diminish available family time. Other parents leave the job of child training to the Sunday School or the day school, erroneously assuming the children's teachers can accomplish the task.

In 1 Samuel 8:3, we learn that Samuel had greedy and unjust sons; some have surmised that it was Samuel's circuit-riding responsibilities that led him to neglect his training of them. Psalm 78 is very instructive concerning not concealing the lessons of ancient times from our children (v.2–6) and recounting God's law to them so they will "set their hope in God, and not forget the works of God, but keep His commandments" (v.7). Hebrews 12:10,11 speaks of the resulting righteous living that comes from receiving the Lord's chastening and instruction.

You may have a battle in one or more of these areas every minute you spend with your child. In one day you make hundreds of decisions as a parent about what you will or will not set as a standard or boundary to give order to your child's life, whether or not you will take action against disobedience, and whether or not you will take time to instruct and teach.

Understanding that you are ordained by God to have authority over your children and being willing to obey His command to discipline your children, through character training and verbal instruction and reproof, will give you confidence in this important task.

Chapter 2

Discipline: The Foundation for Godly Character

Critics of the Word of God have often characterized Biblical child training as harsh or unloving and tending to stifle creativity. Some have said it is merely an opportunity for adult self-interest, that parents who are strict simply want to keep up the appearance of having good kids. They distort the old Puritan view of the child, characterizing it as one that treats the child as inferior and his interests as unimportant. The clearest example of secularists' contempt for the Bible is seen in their condemnation of Christians who use corporal punishment—calling it child abuse.

The child's character—that is, his inner person—must be trained to become mature. Because of the Fall, that inner character tends toward immaturity, foolishness, self-importance, and autonomy, or self-lordship. God put restraints on man in his directives for family government.

Children learn self-government by habitually submitting to parental training. The obedience is to be "in all things" (Colossians 3:20) because this is God's command (Ephesians 6:1–3).[1] This discipline within the family gives you "the ability to do a thing when you don't feel like it right now, and training which produces that ability."[2] The secular expert who denies God does not recognize family government. Stripping the parent of his authority, he puts the child in bondage to himself. Consequently, anarchy reigns within the home, for lawless family government is as destructive as lawless civil government.

The denial of the character-training function of the family is having terrible effects on our society. Ask any employer of young people. Not only are many young adults functionally illiterate, but they are of such foolish character that they cannot be trusted to carry out the simplest of tasks. The value of character training, which builds self-discipline, cannot be over-emphasized.

A noted author states:

[E]ven without regeneration, Christian discipline accomplishes much. We know that in 1815 the average age of criminals in the U.S. was 45; it took a person some years, however unregenerate, to throw off the discipline of the then universal Christian schooling. On the other hand, adults who today are converted but have a background of undisciplined home and school life usually have an insuperable handicap to overcome. A man who can barely read and write, and whose ability to organize and order his life is almost nil, becomes, when converted, a redeemed child of God, but a very ineffective one.[3]

The Bible teaches that character training is a blessing! Psalm 94:12,13 states: "Blessed is the man whom you instruct, O Lord, and teach out of Your law, that you may give him rest from the days of adversity . . ." The Hebrew word for "instruct" in these verses means to chasten or discipline. If you desire to see your children blessed and prospering, you must give them godly character training.

The Bible describes the elements of a good character, elements of belief and conduct in which each child must be trained (See Appendix B). In Scripture, a child with good character is called a "wise child," and characteristic of God's mercy, He blesses with benefits in this life the wise child who accepts discipline.

1. Discipline

A wise child accepts discipline. (See Proverbs 13:1; 15:31–33; Psalm 119:71; Hebrews 5:8,9,14; 1 Samuel 3:19.) A defining characteristic of maturity is acceptance of discipline. In adulthood, it distinguishes the wise man from the fool. When a child accepts correction, he learns—

actually grows intellectually—and becomes more mature. He neither wastes nor despises instruction. It is here that the current teaching on self-esteem is most out of line with Scripture. Parents who attempt—unrealistically or untruthfully—to say only "nice" things to their children do not thereby insure their children will have a positive self-image. It is the child that listens to reproof that accepts himself. He has been taught, from infancy, to know that his sin needs correction and that his parents discipline him to save his life. The child that accepts discipline receives esteem—favor and approval—from God, not from himself.

Start training your child when he is a baby and toddler to accept discipline. When you correct your child or give him a command and he shows anger or ignores your words, he should be spanked. Allowing your little one to throw tantrums (to twist away or throw himself down), or burst into tears, or whine, or to answer "no" when you have corrected him, is the beginning of trouble. Later in childhood, this same child may pout for a long period of time after a spanking or reproof. As a youth, he may make smart retorts, storm out of the room, slam doors, and complain that nobody loves him (not even himself). He becomes a young man who truly "despises" himself (Proverbs 15:32).

Set your heart to be firm and consistent

about teaching your children to accept discipline. The Scriptures teach the principle that maturity comes through accepting godly discipline. "So Samuel grew, and the Lord was with him" (1 Samuel 3:19). (See also Luke 1:80, 2:40,52.) As a result, you will have peace in your home and the joy of seeing your children seek their esteem from God and mature in wisdom and confidence.

2. Obedience

A wise child obeys all commands. This trait might be treated as a joke if we did not have the Word of God as its source. Colossians 3:20 is God's command to children: "Children, obey your parents in all things, for this is well pleasing to the Lord." As some commentators have noted, the child's first opportunity to do God's will is to obey his parents. Yes, your child is a sinner and not perfect, but his heart is to be set on obeying your every command. In this he will please God.

It is your responsibility to train your child to obey you. Start when your baby is very small and begins to respond to your voice. A young baby can be taught to obey your commands, beginning with learning the meaning of "no." Do not mistake volume for tone. Children should learn to obey the word "no" because of its meaning, not because of how loudly it is shouted. There will be a time when that little one discovers that hands can touch and grab all kinds of interesting things. Firmly, but gently, remove the tiny hand and in a negative tone of voice say, "No." There is almost a one hundred percent guarantee the hand will go back to the forbidden object. Flick the back of the little hand with your thumb and middle finger (a snap that stings) and say, "No," again. This will usually produce a startled look and a "hurt feelings" cry from the baby. Use your tone of voice to reassure the baby, saying, "No, you cannot pull on Mommy's glasses."

The attention span of a six- to twelve-month-old baby is short and he will usually go merrily on to something else. Expect him during this time, however, to start to show determination about what he plans to touch and do, a determination that will become more pronounced as he begins to crawl or walk. If you have used your voice to set standards ("No, do not touch," "No, do not scream," etc.), your child will now respond to you when you set boundaries.

When our son learned to crawl, I taught him not to crawl into the kitchen when I was cooking. He would sit and play at the very edge of the carpeted doorway and never "cross the line" because he knew that "no" meant "stop." However, there was a bookcase containing a certain book that had an appealing dust jacket. He loved to tear the book jacket—just ever so slightly—any chance he could get. The bookcase was a "no," the boundary was set, but without fail he went there whenever I was not looking. The "no" and the flicking on the hand were not sufficient. We graduated to spankings because he was dedicated to paying that book a visit every day for a few days in a row. But some spankings—and one ragged dust jacket—later, he learned to not touch anything in that bookcase. This baby, from nine months to eighteen months old, learned so much control about not touching forbidden things that he could be trusted to never get in a cupboard or drawer. (And at the time we lived in a house totally without cabinet doors!)

As your child learns to walk, he should be expected to follow your simple commands, such as, "Johnny, pick up your hat," or, "Johnny, come here." Do not repeat the command over and over without taking action. If you are heard and understood, your little one has no excuse not to respond to your first request. He should be spanked immediately if he does not respond, and then required to do what he did not do the first time. Do not be afraid to interrupt your child to ask him to help or do something for you. The concept that the child should not be interrupted is another ridiculous idea given to us by the "experts."

When your child begins to speak, teach him to respond to your requests with "Yes, sir," or "Yes, Mother," in a pleasant tone. To teach him to do this, give him a command: "Johnny, pick up the toys and put them in the box." Then have him answer and repeat after you, "Yes, Mother, (Ma'am or Mommy), I would be glad to." No child—at any age—should ever be allowed to respond with a whine or a murmur against a command. Even an older child should be expected to do what you ask without being given a long explanation why. Parents who complain about teenagers with smart mouths—who will not do even simple household chores without complaining—usually have brought their woes upon themselves. For years that same child has probably not had to cheerfully obey all commands.

U NFORTUNATELY, many people view the follies or lusts of youth as one of the developmental stages through which all young people must pass.

While an older youth is developing his ability to reason, he still must give his parents the honor due them when he is given a direct command. During this time, it is important to remind the youth that he is disobedient to God if he disobeys you. He must realize that God has given you the authority to request anything of him and to permit or forbid a particular activity, as seems best to you (Hebrews 12:9,10). Accordingly, as the child progressively matures, he may ask permission to do certain things. Respectful questioning should evoke open discussion about the Biblical standards for our lives. Parents should not state that their answer is based on "because I said so," or "because that's just the way it is," but should give clear reasons based on God's commands , that is, "because God has said . . ."

3. Wisdom

A wise child replaces foolishness (youthful lusts) with wisdom and good conduct. Foolishness, or folly, greatly displeases God. The Proverbs give many warnings about the life of a fool—a life that always brings shame and dishonor. Unfortunately, many people view the follies or lusts of youth as one of the developmental stages through which all young people must pass. The Bible, however, teaches that foolishness is part of the fallen character of the child and should be dealt with accordingly.

In fact, the specific rendering of Proverbs 22:15 says that foolishness is strongly anchored, as if by chains, in the heart of a child, but the rod of discipline will drive it far from him. It is your duty as a parent to remove your child's foolishness from him with the rod: God's Word tells your child that he is to flee from foolishness. Foolishness is not cute and is nothing to wink at in a child; an old fool is even more unbearable than a young one. Synonyms for foolishness or folly are: weakness, silliness, imbecility, absurdity, madness, imprudence, misconduct, fatuity, simplicity, weak-mindedness, and shallowness. Webster's dictionary of 1828 says folly is "lack of sense; weakness of intellect; want of understanding." Proverbs is replete with pithy word-pictures describing the fool's way of life.

Much foolishness goes unrecognized today because people have embraced ideas that came to us with the youth rebellion that advocate a relaxation of standards of conduct. In fact, modern child psychology does not recognize foolishness at all, because the child is seen as basically good. Countless excuses are offered for his bad behavior. Some say he is "disabled" or "special" (he has a short attention span or has learning disabilities). Others say his problems are a result of "allergies" (he ate too much sugar, or oats, etc.). He may be excused because of physical tiredness or slight illness. Most commonly, he is excused because he is going through a stage. However, the rebellious behavior that man excuses God calls foolishness, and He has given parents the responsibility to deal with it.

Training a child to be responsible for his actions does much to drive foolishness out, and accepting responsibility for assigned tasks trains the intellect of the child.

Your baby should be taught to become more and more self-controlled. Boisterous behavior and poor manners, whether at the table, in conversation, or elsewhere, should be replaced with acceptable conduct and good manners. We will address these issues more specifically in the chapter on manners.

Foolish talk should be controlled and gradually replaced with sensible speech. Children are prone to silliness. Empty-headed talking and jesting can easily turn into immodest, loose talk or absurd babblings. Over-use of slang words is also a troublesome problem. For example, many children (and adults as well) have a difficult time describing their excitement about something—or the merits of anything, for that matter—without using words such as "neat" or "cool" numerous times. Expect your children to use worthwhile language when they converse and require them to use descriptive vocabulary when explaining something. Do not settle for "Mom, we saw a neat rainbow." Help them to describe it, by asking, "What size was it? What colors did you see? Were they distinct or faint? Did you see a portion of a rainbow or a full arch?" Ask them what makes it so "neat." Teach your children that God holds us accountable for our every word.

There is a danger today that foolishness may be nurtured by an unsuspected source: the church youth group. If we want to see any real reformation in our culture through the institution of the family, we must restore to the family the responsibility of ministering to youth. In many churches—but by no means in all—the purpose of the youth group is founded on premises that are an impediment to the training of godly children. Some of these false premises are:

1) that young people need a place where their problems are understood—where others of the same age share the same struggles; 2) that as it is often difficult for parents to communicate with and understand their teenagers, a youth leader who can identify with the young people is needed; 3) that it is important for young people to have fun and to see that "church people" have fun, too; and 4) that a youth group is needed to reach unsaved youth, and by getting them involved in fun activities, they will be more receptive to the presentation of the Gospel.

Following the trends of secular culture, age-segregated groups have been established in church educational programs. Christopher Schlect, in his book Critique of Modern Youth

Ministry, explains that the "divisions breed immaturity because they hinder younger people from associating with and learning from their elders."[4] The group can become the source of authority, thus diminishing the authority of the father and mother.

The youth group may dictate the rules of conduct, and provide security in place of the parents. The opinions and perspectives of the youth leader may take precedence over that of the father, particularly if the youth see him as being "on their level," and understanding their needs. (A dilemma for the godly youth leader is that if he has made an effort to become a "pal," and then tries to truly direct the group into paths to maturity, his popularity—and thus his authority—may be diminished. The youth will perceive him as they perceive their parents, as not understanding their problems.)

Another danger of youth groups is that they can become focused on a perpetual pursuit of play, which is an "appeal to a sin which is common to youth: fun before duty."[5] The Bible teaches that work and rest are the course for the mature man. In fact, play is not spoken of favorably. Is laughter evil? By no means. But how long would many youth groups survive if their lifeblood was disciplined study and productive work? Not long, because too often escape from maturity and responsibility is the main focus and direction of youth ministries.

According to Proverbs 7:1–4, children are to be dependent upon their parents' teaching. Parents are to be the confidants of their children; their closest friends are to be their father's precepts and teachings. As your children grow, hold to God's precepts for child rearing. Many obedient, loving children change completely during their teenage years and become aloof and rebellious simply because their parents have accepted the current secular theories about "the teenage years" and have neglected responsible leadership in their homes.

CHRISTIANS often don't
recognize the far-reaching
effects of evolutionary thinking.

Do not relinquish your authority to church and other youth groups in the name of fun, or without thoroughly investigating the purposes and activities of the group. Be aware that the youth group can be a contributing cause of the breakdown of family government as ordained by God. If your church youth group operates in any of the ways described above, it may not be the place for your children.

Make your home the center of joyous family activity: invite your neighbors and friends (as families) to share your bounty. In this way you will be able to continue to train your children during the important days just before they take on the responsibilities of adulthood.

What a joy a wise child is to his mother and father! He has become strong in character, prudent, sensible, discerning, intelligent, industrious, informed, and forward-thinking—because his parents were diligent about driving foolishness out of him and training him for mature living.

4. Devotion to God

A wise child is mindful of his Creator and learns to know and value God's Word. (Ecclesiastes 12:1; 1 Timothy 4:12; 2 Timothy 3:15.) Christians often don't recognize the far-reaching effects of evolutionary thinking. This point of view has literally permeated every area of our lives. It is vitally important that your child come to know and believe in God our Creator at a very early age. It will give him an awareness of God's presence and loving care. It also gives even the small child a sense of his calling. God made the earth for His glory. It is to be filled with people, subdued, replenished, and ruled by them. We must teach our children to be mindful of their Creator's work and God's purposes for giving them life.

Even when the child is in the womb, the mother's praise, thanksgiving, and worship minister to him because God inhabits the praise of His people. From birth onward, read God's Word aloud and pray with your child. When he discovers the created works of God, turn his thoughts toward God: "Look at these nice little toes God gave you!"; "What a beautiful flower God made for us!" Young, maturing minds should be warned early of the deception and violence of Satan against God's perfect creation. They should learn to recognize the many ramifications of evolutionary thinking, according to their ability. As they mature, it is important to call attention to printed or spoken bias toward evolution in the news media and educational materials.

Train your child in stewardship. Even the very young toddler must learn to respect and care for the things God has given him. He can begin by learning not to throw trash around or mar grandma's dining room table and chairs with toys. Household chores, which teach orderly and tidy living, should be started as soon as the child can walk. Gardening and yard work, helping to repair broken items and maintain possessions, learning to keep tools and equipment in working order, and building and making items with one's own hands are all necessary aspects of becoming a good steward. When a child learns to care for the property God has given him, he shows gratitude to his Creator. He is serving his Creator with his best days, while he is young and full of energy.

5. Knowledge of God

Of course, learning to know the Creator requires that the child know the God of the Bible. Today there seems to be a distaste for doctrine—or what is actually the teachings of Scripture. The church has taken on the thinking of the world and is very "me" centered. How you feel about God is stressed rather than whether you are indeed worshipping Him in spirit and in truth, an attitude that is reflected in much of today's so-called Christian literature for children that teaches very little truth.

In contrast, the young Timothy (like so many others in bygone generations) was saturated with the Word of God. His mother found no excuses for herself in that spiritually divided home. Her faith was pure and she made certain her son learned God's Word and conformed his life to it (1 Timothy 4:6; 2 Timothy 1:5, 3:15–17).

From the beginning, teach your child the Bible as the Word of God. Teach him that it is God's revelation of Himself, in His Son and in His people. Most of contemporary Bible literature for children follows the fairy tale method:

the stories focus on individuals and conclude with a moral application. Some writers of Sunday school curriculum have followed this same approach and, as a result, often we have little more than a Gospel Romper Room taking place on Sunday morning.

S.G. DeGraaf, in his four-volume series *Promise and Deliverance* (which we highly recommend for every Christian home library) offers an excellent discourse on the issue of Bible story-telling. He states:

"Every time you tell one of these [Bible] stories, you are telling about God. And you must tell not only what God did but also how He revealed Himself through His actions . . ."

If we set aside no time for quiet reflection before telling the Bible story but simply follow the most natural course, we will find ourselves talking of men and their actions, of what they believed and how they sinned. God still enters the picture, of course; He intervenes now and then and offers rewards and punishments. Before we know it, we arrive at the "moral" of the story. We tell the children that God will deal with them according to their actions; if they are 'good,' He will rewards them, but if they are 'bad,' He will punish them.

I venture to say that this is by far the most popular way of telling Bible stories to children

. . . But while some people think that this procedure keeps the story simple and direct, they forget they are not passing on what we are told in Scripture, the record of God's self-revelation . . .

In other words, every story in Scripture reveals something of the counsel of God for our redemption, even though every story tells it differently. And in every story God is the prime agent, revealing Himself through His acts as the Redeemer. The entire work of redemption can be seen in each story.

Consider the story of Joseph as an example. We could focus on the wicked brothers and on Joseph, who put his trust in God and was in turn saved by God. But when we do so, we are omitting an element that forms an actual part of the Scripture record: it was God who sovereignly brought all these things to pass in order to preserve the life of a great people. Now let's tell the story again from the latter point of view. From the very beginning, God and His people become our main concern. In a certain sense, Joseph becomes secondary—a mere instrument.[6]

DeGraaf's comments give us much to consider. Is the Bible a book about the history of man—man on center stage—or is it "His-story"? It is a sad truth that our children often come away from hearing a Bible story knowing little about God and a great deal about the texture and color of Joseph's coat.

Beyond a knowledge of Bible history, however, every child needs to know the doctrines of his faith. Unfortunately, catechizing children has fallen by the wayside. Many evangelical parents go so far as to think a catechism is un-Christian, or believe it represents cold and lifeless religion. The word "catechize" comes from the Greek, kata (thoroughly) and echein (to sound), meaning a thorough, close, or searching questioning. Thus, a very important aspect of Christian child training is teaching your child the tenets of Christian belief and then thoroughly questioning him concerning his understanding of those beliefs. The error is not in catechizing a child, but in leading a child to believe he is saved thereby. There are quality children's catechisms available. Be certain to use one that notes the Scripture sources so that your child learns that God's Word teaches these truths.

It is not for parents to question whether their children will be saved and be among the elect. This is not our work, but God's alone. However, God makes no exception for children under the covenant. All are to be taught what it means to love the Lord. We are to teach them to know the Scriptures that "are able to make [them] wise for salvation through faith which is in Christ Jesus" (2 Timothy 3:15) and trust God that we will see our children's children prospering in God's kingdom (Psalm 128).

6. Respect for Authority

The wise child honors and reveres (or fears) parents and elders of authority (Exodus 20:12; Leviticus 19:3,32; Deuteronomy 5:16; Ephesians 6:2,3).

Many evangelicals believe that the law of God contained in the Ten Commandments is not binding on us today. This error has had far-reaching effects on all aspects of life, but we are concerned here with how disregard for the Ten Commandments has contributed to the destruction of the family. We note that the Apostle Paul, in his instruction to the New Testament church, restated the Fifth Commandment as valid and binding:

Honor your father and your mother, that your days may be long upon the land which the Lord your God is giving you (Exodus 20:12).

Children, obey your parents in the Lord: for this is right. 'Honor your father and mother,' which is the first commandment with promise: 'that it may be well with you and you may live long on the earth (Ephesians 6:1–3).

God has established a law—order for man. Without it, the result is lawlessness and anarchy. Literally, man cannot live without God's law-order. There are various authorities instituted by

God and the authority of parents is primary. It has been wisely said, "If parents are not obeyed by children, no other authority will be honored or obeyed."[7] We can see how crucial this character trait is to a nation.

The "adolescent syndrome" of our culture is a result of a revolt against authority. The wisdom and knowledge of past generations was considered "out of it" by the youth of the sixties. Addressing this issue, a noted commentator points out the absurdity of trying to throw out the past; after all, children inherit life, wisdom, and experience from their elders, including the very things that they need for survival, such as buildings for shelter.[8] The ability of one generation to improve, build upon, and surpass the accomplishments of the former generation is dependent upon the respect of youth for parental authority.

In the sixties disrespect for the older generation was fostered on many fronts: parents, teachers, and others in that age group did not deserve obedience, it was maintained, because they were hypocrites.[9] All sorts of other reasons were given: the revolt against parental authority was justified by the parents' so-called inability to communicate (otherwise known as "the generation gap") or the parents' materialism. The Bible clearly commands otherwise: Paul said a child must honor and obey because "this is right."

No parent is perfect; all are sinners—even though they may be saved. Parents have not been given authority because they are perfect: they are due certain respect and honor because God has ordained them to that position of authority. It is not due to hypocrisy (as Spock asserted) that we have impotent parents unable to exercise their godly authority, but because they carry the misconception that it is their kindness or good character that makes them worthy of obedience. Parents who are always wavering—constantly wondering whether they should require this or that of their child—do not understand the position that they have been given by God.[10] Parents are to be shown due respect by children by virtue of their God-given calling. The Scripture also teaches that age demands respect; a child's respect for his parents and other elders is to continue into his adult years.

It is important to remember that the honor of authority brings with it the responsibility to be honorable. Fathers are especially reminded of this in Ephesians 6:4. Parents are expected to grow in grace. They should not be harsh or unreasonable, but just; not inconsistent, but reliable; not neglectful, but nurturing and admonishing.

In training the child to respect authority, the Scripture commands the child to "revere [fear] his mother and his father" (Leviticus 19:3). Exodus 20:12 says, "Honor your father and your mother." The commentator Ginsburg explains what these terms meant to the Jew:

> The expression "fear" . . . include[s] the following: (1) not to stand or sit in the place set apart for the parents; (2) not to carp at [find fault] or oppose their statements; and (3) not to call them by their proper names, but either call them father or mother, or my master, my lady. Whilst the expression "honor" . . . include[s] (1) to provide them with food and raiment, and (2) to escort them. The parents . . . are God representatives upon earth hence as God is both to be "honored" with our substance (Proverbs 3:9), and as He is to be "feared" (Deuteronomy 6:13), so our parents are both to be "honored" (Exodus 20:12) and "feared" (19:3); and as he who blasphemed the name of God is stoned (29:16), so he who curses his father or mother is stoned (20:9).[11]

As soon as your baby begins to speak he should be taught to honor and fear you with his words. He must not be allowed to call your name or ask for attention in demanding tones. The modern fad to have children call their parents by their first names—supposedly to help them "become friends" with their children—springs from the revolt against Godly authority. God did not command us to be friends (buddies or pals) with our children, but to exercise godly authority over them and to be parents to them.

IF CHILDREN are constantly waited on or served, they not only do not learn necessary life skills, but they also do not learn to honor adults.

Neither younger nor older children should be allowed to contradict or correct parents and elders. Such behavior is a sign of disrespect and lack of reverence; in the "old days" it was termed "getting too familiar." When children are too familiar with or (lack respect for) their elders, they will no longer seek to gain wisdom through respectful questions and discussions with an elder, and will reveal their pride in their own understanding by making disrespectful, sharp retorts.

In matters of seating, children are to defer to parents and older people. Boys, especially, should always relinquish their seats to a woman, an older man, or a young girl. Very young children can be taught this courtesy by calling attention to father's "special chair" and making the rule that no one takes his place.

According to the meaning of honor

explained by Ginsburg, young children need to spend much of their time providing help to their parents or serving them. If children are constantly waited on or served, they not only do not learn necessary life skills, but they also do not learn to honor adults.

Teach your children and expect them to pick up dropped items, open doors, carry library books or grocery sacks, and serve you coffee. Teach them that while you care for them now when they are young, God expects them to care for you in your old age. This command has been the most neglected and disregarded because of the cradle-to-grave "care" government now claims to provide. The principle that the older generation reaches forward to help the younger and the younger generations reaches back to help the older is being lost. Many grandparents end their years with feelings of uselessness and loneliness, and must seek help for their physical needs outside their family because of the disregard for this command to honor parents. Our children need to see our obedience to God in our behavior toward our parents so that their generation will know to honor us in our old age.

Since the youth culture surrounding our children is characterized by rebellion and disrespect for elders, it must be a priority of Christian parents to teach their children what the Word of

God says about honor and obedience to parental authority. Young people need to know that God means what He says. This command comes with a promise—we must obey it in order that we may enjoy long life and that we may prosper in the land which the Lord our God gives us (Deuteronomy 5:16).

Chapter 3

THE ROD OF DISCIPLINE

*T*HE BIBLE TEACHES *that the rod is to be used to chasten or discipline a child (Proverbs 13:24). It is the implement God gave to the parent authority to enforce His commands. Many parents erroneously view the rod as negative—a last resort to be used when all else fails. This view is not a Scriptural one, but a humanistic one. The word "chastening" is used in both Testaments: paideuō in Greek and yâcar in Hebrew, meaning the disciplinary correction used to train a child. The meanings of both include to inflict pain by blows, to scourge, punish, correct, instruct, control.*

The Word of God views chastening with the rod as restorative (Proverbs 19:18; 23:14; Hebrews 12:11). The purpose of spanking is to reclaim an offender. This concept is included in Webster's 1828 dictionary, which defines "chasten" in this way: "to correct by punishment; to punish; to inflict pain for the purpose of reclaiming an offender." When your child disregards or disobeys your command, he breaks fellowship with you and offends you as his God-ordained authority.[12] This estrangement must be corrected and made right again by use of the rod. When properly administered a spanking is not a negative, destructive attack on your child's life, but a positive, peacemaking mission!

The Bible says that the child is part of this fallen race and that he is born a sinner (Psalm 51:5; Romans 5:12). Parents must realize that chastening is necessary because of the child's sin nature and must recognize bad behavior for what it is—sin. In Otto J. Scott's article, "The Definition of Sin," we are reminded that "sin is more than an act; it is the condition of man's heart, mind, and being."

REAL CHILD ABUSE is allowing a child to be overtaken by the destructive forces of sin and rebellion.

He states further, "Christians once held very clear perceptions about the nature, attributes, and patterns of sin. Sin was categorized, defined, understood . . . The seven deadly, or capital, sins were once taught to school children, and drilled into every consciousness. These deadly seven, from which all other sins flow, were considered fatal to spiritual growth. Those who fell into their snares knew, at least, the nature of their trap. They did not blame their parents. The seven are: pride, lust, greed, covetousness, gluttony, envy, and sloth . . ." [13]

The serious error of humanistic child psychology is that the child is viewed as a cute curiosity-seeker. His troubles are said to come from his environment or are accepted as part of the developmental stages through which he must pass on the way to self-discovery. The truth is that because of the Fall every child is born self-centered and totally dedicated to self-rule. From the beginning he is on the path to destruction (Genesis 8:21). The sin nature mars each child as the image-bearer of God, and he can only be fully restored through regeneration by God's Spirit and the blood of Jesus Christ. But even before the child acknowledges his salvation in Christ, God provides a restraint on his sin nature through godly discipline.

Chastening enables parents to control and give order to their child's life; there is restraint on his foolish sin nature (Proverbs 22:15; 10:13). Chastening truly is a life-saver for the child (Proverbs 23:14). Secularists claim that spanking is child abuse, but the real child abuse is allowing a child to be overtaken by the destructive forces of sin and rebellion within his own heart (Proverbs 23:13,14; 29:15; 19:18). Parents must realize that God ordained them to have the "power of the rod" to bring the child into obedience to their authority, instead of his own stubborn self-will and self-authority. Thus, the child's personal life, as well as that of his family, is made peaceful.

Throughout this book there is reference to administering spankings for disobedience. The Bible teaches us how to use the rod. First, the rod in Scripture is a thin stick (Proverbs 23:13,14; 22:15; 29:15; 10:13), what we call a "switch." It has a definite sting but it does not injure the body organs or structure as a larger, heavier wooden object could. We are not to injure our child. That is wickedness! Never use objects that could damage your child.

Secondly, the spanking must produce sufficient pain. Use the rod on the backside and on the bare skin (to produce a sting), not through layers of clothing (Proverbs 10:13). Loud crying is not always an indication of pain, because some children begin quite a wail and produce tears easily before they have even had one swat. Do not withhold the amount of spanking needed because of crying, or put off using the rod because you do not want to make him cry, or stop administering spankings because they do not seem to make any difference (Proverbs 19:18, 23:13,14).

Require your child to maintain control of himself. Do not allow him to be theatrical (e.g., scream, throw a fit, kick, gag, cough, or try to vomit). If he throws a tantrum, tell him his tantrum will result in another spanking.

Thirdly, the Bible makes no exception for different personalities. Even your quiet child has a fallen nature, though he may manifest it differently than your aggressive child. All your children need spankings for their rebellion: some just need them more often.

In keeping with the Biblical view that chastening is a restorative act, no time of correction is complete without the child being given the opportunity to renew his joyful relationship with his parents. Following the example of our Heavenly Father (Jeremiah 31:18–20; Psalm 89:27–33), we can discern a pattern:

1. Chastening by the father (always including punishment and determining the restitution or consequences, Psalm 99:8).

2. Repentance of the child (confession of fault, asking forgiveness).

3. Restoration to a right standing with the father (forgiveness by father, followed by renewed joy and acts of restitution by child).

The Fabrizios have explained this process as administering the spanking, explaining the wrong, requiring the child to repent and to correct his error, and enfolding the repentant child with loving arms, assuring him of God's forgiveness.[14]

Some common questions arise: "When should a spanking be given?" or "What actions warrant giving a spanking?" Basically, any action or attitude that defies your authority; a disobedience to your commands, and foolish conduct or rebellion (self-will, stubbornness, and anger, i.e., tantrums) are reasons to administer a spanking, because all are willful acts and attitudes against your commands.

Before you chasten with the rod, your child must be taught your law. This was briefly covered in the previous chapter in the discussion about teaching the meaning of the word "no." It is your responsibility to establish standards for your children. Many parents of young children become frustrated because they feel they spend most of their time saying "no" and giving spankings, especially from the age of two to three years. The tempting solution is to not set so many boundaries, so you will not have to chasten so often. Besides, you may rationalize, the spankings do not seem to "get through," so you resort to humanistic thinking and blame it on the "terrible twos" (or "threes" or . . .). Be assured, your child is not going through some developmental stage, he is a young sinner in need of chastening and teaching (discipline). If you are a parent of a toddler or young child, recognize the source of your discouragement and temptation to compromise: your adversary, who roams about seeking whom he may devour.

Another popular false instruction concerns the kind of voice used in training children. Parents are warned and scolded about being certain their voices are just right when they speak to their children. They are told they must keep a special sweet ring to it, that this negotiating tone will convince the child to do the good thing. Nonsense! It is disgraceful to hear a grown man putting on his "I'm afraid you're not going to like me" voice when negotiating with a two-year-old about whether the child should button his coat or not.

Children should be taught to respond to a reproving tone or look and the "no" words or phrases. Obviously, we must be controlled by the Spirit and not lose control of our voices and words by saying abusive things. But we will not always be so, and when we do sin against the

Lord and our child, we must confess it to the Lord and our wronged child. However, when you mean "no," your voice should sound like it. To mix a sing-song sweet tone with a serious reproof only confuses your child and gives him an opportunity for disobedience.

One final caution concerning the command for parents to chasten with the rod. There is a general tendency in our times toward pragmatism—doing what works. The problem with choosing a method or means just because it gets results is that this is not God's way. Some have argued that sending a child to his room to think changes his bad behavior. Another common practice is for parents to distract their toddler, diverting his attention to something else when he is doing something wrong. For many parents the bottom line is, "Isn't it all right to use a number of different methods besides spanking, as long as they solve the problem?" That is precisely what other methods do not do: they do not solve the problem. Problems—or sin—cannot be remedied any way other than God's way. God clearly states that childish sin is to be corrected with the chastening rod. For a parent to do otherwise is sin against the command of God.

Chapter 4

TEACHING WISE CONDUCT
AND GOOD MANNERS

*I*F YOU ARE OF THE CURRENT *generation of young parents—those with a birthdate sometime after 1940—you are working under a great handicap. Those who were parents prior to W.W.II were able to rely on a great reserve of religious tradition. Although the changes in child rearing actually began to take place much earlier—that is, in the early 1800s—the Biblical view of the child and belief in parental authority were still widely held well into this century. However, as the new views of the child became indoctrinated into every school student by the social engineers, the government schools, and eventually America's Sunday schools, child training became a totally different undertaking.*

No one was too concerned until the arrival of the hippie generation. Then Dr. Spock rushed in to tell mothers and fathers of that obnoxious generation that they were hypocrites and were being too hard on these pure, honest "love-children." What he failed to confess in the sixties—and later—was that it was his radically new definitions of children and authority that he had preached for the previous twenty years that had helped to rip away the last vestiges of the traditional views of childrearing. It was Dr. Spock and his contemporaries, and many before them, who had proclaimed a new methodology—a scientific and "better" way of child rearing.[15]

Perhaps you object, saying that you have not been affected by the new philosophy, as you did not join the counterculture movement. (This would be to your advantage, since nothing of true value came of the sixties youth rebellion.) However, we all have been affected—and infected—along with the dedicated converts. To some degree our thinking has been altered about authority, law, the depravity of man, the nature of sin, and the source of sin. In fact, though we think we do not appreciate much of the Bohemian lifestyle of that dropout generation, we have in fact altered our manners and rules to fit the new standard. This is the erosion and death of Western culture. It is to our shame that we somehow feel spiritual about not having any rules about much of anything. Manners? Courtesy? They make you appear stuffy and too formal! We must be "free" and relaxed with one another: let the "real you" show so we can have a real relationship. Supposedly, the more unmannered and uncouth we are, the more easily Christian love can flow between us: we have torn down all false barriers. All of this is, of course, wrong thinking. I do not really love my neighbor if I force him to take me at my worst at all times. The real me is a sinner—perhaps regenerate, but still in need of God's discipline on my character. When I am always allowed to "just be myself," I may not be much of a neighbor.

There is a need to revive the manners and courtesy practiced in former times. Deceitful historians and psychologists of earlier days have led us to believe that rules of etiquette and other kinds of manners were stifling. Some would even have us believe that such strictness damaged people for the rest of their lives. It is time that we wise up to the source of these complaints: often, the preachers against manners were those who favored violent revolution and radical cultural change.

The root cause of unmannerliness is lack of disciplined character, and therein lies the difference between our times and earlier ones. Manners and courtesy were an intrinsic part of a much more disciplined society. Generally speaking, the observance of various social customs and manners was seen as a kindness to others. It is a selfish, self-centered person that revolts against rules of conduct. The well-mannered person has a self-controlled, disciplined character and receives respect from those with whom he lives, whether in private or public life. His concern is that his conduct does not take advantage of or exploit his neighbor's person or possessions, for this is theft. The disciplined man is the one who obeys God's great commandment: He loves the Lord, obeys His law, and loves his neighbor as himself. Thus the commandments—which, when obeyed are manifested in us as the fruit of the Spirit—give the outline of inner character and outward conduct (manners) for child training. This should be kept in mind as you consider the advice that follows.

All of God's law sets forth our duty toward Him. The first four commands define for us who God is (His character and His attributes), what we must believe about Him, and how we must respond to Him. The final six are also to be seen in relation to our duty toward God: they give us His governing Word defining what it means to love our family and our neighbor. In training up our children in God's law as He commanded, we must always be aware, and also teach our children, that obedience to parents is first of all God-pleasing. The primary motive of our discipline should be to bring about obedience to God.

The child's loving acts toward family and neighbors should be motivated by his desire to please God: only as the child loves and pleases God can he love his family and his neighbor. This is the point at which the philosophy of altruism is in error. Altruism is the humanistic view that man determines his actions by what pleases others; it is man-centered morality and it is ungodly. Many secular educators and child psychologists embrace this philosophy and are leading many astray with it. When you hear such buzz words as "brotherhood," "the altruistic child," "the good of society," and "getting along with your neighbor," recognize that you are hearing the language of the philosophy of altruism—a philosophy that is not Christian.

The advice in character training and manners contained here is based on and defined by the Law—the Word of God—and not man's vain attempts to bring about brotherhood by making his own rules of conduct.

Piety or Holy Living

The first and foremost responsibility of Christian parents is to train their children to love God and obey His commands. This is most impressively done when parents themselves love God and attend to personal holiness. Because they are sinners, parents are not perfect; they not only make terrible mistakes, but they are also inconsistent and many times neglect to do what they should do. God did not stipulate that the right to teach a child about Him is conditional, that it depends on a parent's perfection. The command was based on the character of God and His laws. He is always faithful and true, but we are not. Deuteronomy 6:1–9 promises blessing for those who practice His law; His law is to be taught to children and they will be blessed with long life. It is self-deception to believe my perfection will convince my child to love God. It is the call of God on the child, through the power of the Holy Spirit, by the regeneration of the Word, that saves the child. Thus, it should be a daily task, not just a Sunday task, to teach and indoctrinate our children in the Scriptures.

We must not make the mistake of the pietists, who see life as being divided into a secular—and hence, for the Christian, evil—side and a spiritual side. This dualistic view of life has been a major reason for the salt losing its savor. It also flies in the face of God's great command to love the Lord your God with all your heart and soul and mind. A child who receives teaching about God for only a few minutes on Sunday, a grace at meal times, and some bedtime prayers thrown in at night is being reared in the pietist tradition. The Word of God has little impact on or direction for how he views those parts of his life not related to prayers and church attendance. The law of God has no authority over the secular areas and is not applied to his everyday life. Growing up with this view of holiness, he may, with great striving and anxiety, try to stretch his spiritual activity to longer and longer periods, believing this is what true holiness is.

We must, instead, understand that true holiness is realizing that this is God's world and that he is the Ruler of all things—that He is the King over heart and life. Holiness requires that we think His thoughts after Him and that we be certain that everything we do brings Him glory. The chief end of man is to glorify and enjoy God forever.

Even our youngest children must learn to know God in this way. Parents must teach their children to be mindful of their Creator; a good place to begin is with the story of redemption— from Genesis to Revelation. Children must become thoroughly acquainted with the Word of God, which can be accomplished by consistent Bible reading and Bible storytelling. Young children should memorize portions of Scripture on a regular basis. This discipline builds knowledge of God's Word and prepares the intellect for learning to read and other academic studies. Loving God requires purity of heart, humility, and meekness. In chastening and disciplining your child, there will be many opportunities for you to teach him about and help him practice these qualities of holy living. He must learn to speak the truth, to denounce his pride, and be teachable under your authority.

It is a good practice to read, discuss, and pray about the Proverbs with him from around five years of age through his teen years. Each verse provides a case study or life application of the Law of God. It gives fathers a perfect occasion to apply the Word of God to the everyday life of the family. One chapter can be read per calendar date and each child can choose one verse to be explained and discussed. As the family prays together at the end, God is asked to make those things true in this family.

One great lack among evangelical Christians today is the pursuit of a Christian mind. We are not renewing our minds and, as a result, we are being conformed to the world system (Romans 12:1,2). If we are going to teach our children about holiness, we must learn it ourselves. The Bible teaches us the correct view of everything from economics to governments, from foreign policy to duties of mothers and fathers. Yet few pulpits are teaching it and fewer individuals have bothered to read and study the Word concerning these issues of life. Holiness means we will plug our ears to the anti-Christian media and education and open our ears to God and let His Word speak. Every parent must be a student of truth and strive to take every thought captive to Christ Jesus. Every part of a child's day, whether he is learning how to get along with others, or studying history, or learning to do his chores, or listening to discussions of current events in the world, should be from God's perspective. This is true piety and holy living.

Courtesy in Speech

Being polite to others shows kindness and respect. The words, "Pardon me?" or "Excuse me?" can be taught with the child's first words. The responses, "Whaaat?" or "Huh?" make one seem coarse—and even dimwitted.

"Please" and "Thank you" should be required of the little toddler with every request he makes. "Drink, please" is sufficient for the beginner. When he is able to say short sentences, he should be taught to ask, "May I have a drink?" (Not, "Can I?") The little child who learns to make requests politely speaks respectfully. His mother will not be ordered around as if she were a short-order cook.

It is rude (and selfish) to interrupt others who are speaking. A little child can be very demanding. He is born thinking and acting as though the world revolves around him. He must learn to control his wants and respect others. Teach your child not to interrupt others when they are speaking. If his reason is very important, such as a necessary trip to the potty or someone is in need of help, he should say quietly, "Excuse me." You should then recognize his polite interruption and give him your attention. A child should be taught to communicate his bathroom needs in a quiet whisper: he should not make an announcement to the whole grocery store or roomful of people. The rule of not interrupting should apply to all conversations in which he takes part: he must take his turn to tell Daddy about his exciting day, waiting patiently until his sister finishes her story.

Rudeness can also be a problem when mothers are conversing on the phone: some children make this an opportunity to interrupt mother with frivolous talk or to be boisterous or start a fight. This shows lack of self control and deceitful character and, if the child does not control himself after a word of reproof, he should be spanked.

Siblings should practice courtesy with one another. It is just as important that they express regret for clumsily bumping into one another as into an adult. They should also learn to say, "Excuse me," when they need to walk around someone or to pass between two people in the midst of a conversation. Children must learn not to rudely push through crowds, stepping on toes.

In order to teach courtesy to your children, keep them with you in crowds. When parents let their children run free and unattended those children do not learn good public conduct.

A child who has learned to be polite gains respect. He is pleasant to have around because his ways are gentle and the law of kindness is in his heart.

Respect for Life and Property

Children also need to learn reverence for God's gift of life and respect for the possessions He gives us and our neighbors. Reverence for life starts with honor and respect for parents and elders and should be extended to brothers and sisters next. Another casualty of the modern adolescent syndrome is brotherly and sisterly love. Children who are socialized through their years of public education and age-segregated youth groups often develop snobbish attitudes toward the other children in their own families. Younger children are seen as pests or intruders into cliques and secret groups made up of peers. Home-taught brothers and sisters, who work, study, and play together, learn respect for one another. This family love and respect gives children an appreciation for the human life God has created.

Respect for life and property should be extended to friends outside the home during the young adult years before marriage. Christian youths are being set up for disaster because of modern dating customs. The Bible teaches a continuance of the brotherly-sisterly respect for others until the marriage consummation. Young people who are caught in the web of intimacy while dating break God's laws against lying, stealing, committing adultery, and showing disregard for the life of another.[16]

The humanists have carried on a persuasive ad campaign convincing us of the need for socialization. Homeschooling parents have been asked this one question by well meaning people more than any other: "What about your child's socialization?" Of course, what the secular educator and the common person mean by socialization are two different things. We will examine only the common usage here.

Most people, when they express concern about your child's socialization, are referring to what we call social skills—the ability to get along with people. Government school propagandists have convinced us that a child can only learn compassion, tolerance, patience, and congeniality in "neutral" public schools. However, the truth is out—public schools are anything but neutral and seem to be teaching everything but compassion, tolerance, patience, and congeniality. God made the better way: the home is the best place to learn social skills. The child who learns to be gentle with a little brother will be gentle to others; the one who learns to be a peacemaker among his brothers and sisters will know how to be so with others, because he has had to practice respecting the rights of others in the most arduous boot camp of all—the home.

Teach your child to not grab toys from others. When he does, have him return them without a tantrum or angry outburst. If he does not, he should be corrected with the rod, not distracted with another toy.

Never allow bickering and loud arguing between your children to go unchecked. Silence it immediately and require them to speak respectfully to each other, even when solving disagreements. Children must never hit, scratch, or try to hurt each other. Spankings should be given for such conduct. A child should never strike an adult, for it is very shameful in the Lord's eyes.

Many Christians have interpreted God's commands not to covet or steal in such a way that they have come to regard possessions as evil because they believe wealth is forbidden in the Bible. Actually, it is the idolatrous love of riches that the Bible forbids. It is time we realize our view of wealth or property is more the gospel according to Marx than the teaching of Christ the Lord. During the sixties, the counter-culture showed us a new way to view possessions.

Possessions were not to be maintained and preserved but dirtied, abused, and discarded. The more dilapidated your furniture, the less tidy and dirtier your clothes, the more spiritual you were considered to be. How different is this view from that of previous generations, who so carefully crafted items of beauty and usefulness that they could be passed on to future generations. Proper respect results in the preservation and increase of the family inheritance. God requires that we not only respect our own inheritance, but that we neither covet nor steal our neighbor's property.

Toddlers can be taught to care for their toys. They should not use them roughly and should put them away neatly. Many children have too many toys. If we gave them fewer and taught them to keep the few they owned in good condition, the children would be much better off. Outdoor toys and tools should always be put away after play and work and not left in the yard to rust.

As well as learning to care for their own possessions, children should be taught to preserve the family home and furnishings. They should learn not to put shoes on the furniture, for in so doing they will not only greatly extend the life and preserve the beauty of the pieces, but show appreciation for God's gifts and demonstrate respect for the hours father worked to provide them. Many of us do not have brand new furnishings, but that is beside the point. The lesson to be learned is respecting another's goods. A child must learn not to abuse his own possessions and to be careful with the possessions of others.

In a previous chapter we discussed the importance of teaching your baby not to touch everything within his reach. Learning this self-control is so important with respect to other people's possessions. The child who is allowed to feel, grab, squeeze, and open drawers and cupboards at whim will take, destroy, or damage things that do not belong to him. Parents, do you respect the lives and property of others? Then you will train your child to not touch items in stores, in the homes of other people, or anywhere else. Marring or destroying another's possessions is theft, which is sin.

Eating Habits and Table Manners

Poor nutrition in young children is often not the fault of a mother's cooking or a low income, but the result of a lack of discipline. One of the common displays of rebellion against authority is revealed in the eating habits of a baby or a young child. This rebellion is often allowed by concerned parents who have been told that their child will have psychological problems in later life if his self-determined eating habits are opposed. The problem may begin in infancy with the young mother who is rightly convinced about the importance of breast feeding her child, but who mistakenly thinks this means demand feeding. Believing every cry to mean hunger, she ends up breast feeding her baby too often. The baby is stuffed and spits up and cries even more. This is not intended to be either a debate or a medical discussion about breast feeding, but a caution to young mothers to be careful not to set their children up for discipline problems relating to eating habits.

Parents must remember that they are given the responsibility to care for the physical welfare of their children. No ten-month-old, nor two-year-old, nor six-year-old child knows what is best for him to eat. He may decide that bananas and toast are the only thing he wants, but this is not what is best. As the young child is being weaned, he should be introduced to a variety of vegetables, meats, fruits, and grains—but not sweets. Nobody has to be coerced into eating sweets. Unfortunately, in our junk food society, many parents and grandparents make the mistake of teaching the child the habit of snacking on sweets. For a child to acquire a taste for nourishing foods, three rules must be observed: 1) eat all foods that are served, whether they are liked or not; 2) no snacking between meals, especially sweets; and 3) no dessert unless the main meal has been eaten.

There will always be some foods we do not like but we must learn to gratefully accept them as God's provision for us. Train your child to eat foods he does not like by serving him only one small spoonful and requiring him to eat it all. Another key to learning to eat all foods provided is variety: if you serve corn and never peas, that is what your child will like. Violation of the second rule often creates picky eaters. A child who has had a high—energy snack not long before a meal will not feel hungry: somehow potatoes and carrots are just not that appealing after three cookies and a can of pop. If we ignore rule three, we allow the child to be irresponsible and choose the least important food to satisfy his hunger. Eating seems to be one of the battlefields where parental authority is won or lost. Disciplined eating is one of the most misunderstood aspects of child training today.

Table manners are characterized by those who detest the mores of the past as just another excuse on the part of the older generation to stifle free expression. To defend their position, they depict the dinner hour of grandfather's day as a cold, strained, unhappy occasion. While harshness and even cruelty undoubtedly existed in some homes in earlier times—just as it exists today in some homes—we are not thereby warranted in rejecting an essential aspect of good conduct. Good table manners are one of those observances that show our consideration for others.

It should be an established rule that the entire family eats together at the table, without the distraction of television. Hopefully, you have done away with television; if not, it should not be allowed to destroy family meals. Mealtime is to be a time of thankful eating and warm sharing and learning—as well as a time of laughter and storytelling.

Every meal cannot be all bliss. As with other elements of child training, good table manners require instruction, correction, and consistent practice. When babies join the family at mealtime, they may cry. Toddlers may cry because you will not let them bang their spoons, or they may refuse to eat their beans, necessitating a spanking. Moments must be taken to instruct a child how to hold his spoon, and how to use it instead of his fingers. Every meal is a practice session for all the little points of good table manners.

All children should learn the following basic dining courtesies:

1. The table is not an appropriate place for boisterous talk and play. Children should not rudely interrupt adult conversation or act silly.

2. Napkins rather than clothing should be used to wipe hands. Napkins may be spread on the lap when eating begins.

3. Elbows and arms should not rest on the table. Children tend to lie or lean on the table with their heads near their plates. They should learn to sit up straight. One arm should be kept in the lap and the other used to raise the fork and cup to the mouth.

4. Each child should wait to be served or until food is passed to him. Also, he should be instructed to select the top, the nearest, or the smallest serving. The piece first touched should be taken without sorting through the food. When only one serving remains, the child should kindly ask father and mother, then others, if they would like to have it, before he takes it.

5. Reaching across the table or in front of another is rude. The desired item should be requested courteously, "May I please have the bread?" or "Would you please pass the butter," and received with a "Thank you." Serving dishes should be passed around—not across—the table.

6. Chewing with the mouth open, smacking the lips, taking too large bites, slurping drinks, and speaking with food in the mouth are bad habits that should be corrected. Toddlers should not be allowed to play with food or smear it on the high chair tray, the table, or themselves.

7. It is ungrateful and discourteous to pick through food, to complain about it, or to refuse what is served. Children can learn to eat the food that is served without whining. God must always be thanked for His provision and the cook shown appreciation for preparing the meal. Children should thank their mothers before leaving the table—a courtesy that should not be forgotten when eating in other homes.

8. Children should ask to be excused from the table at the end of the meal. They should also request permission if they need to leave the table during the meal. Toddlers and young children should use the toilet and wash their hands before eating. There is no need for children to get up and down from the table. They should stay until the end of the meal, through the time of family fellowship, and then be excused to return to their play.

Courtesy at meals is not something reserved for diplomats and presidents. It is another aspect of self-government that is an act of kindness and respect for others.

Hygiene and Cleanliness

Wherever the Gospel of Christ Jesus and His kingdom has permeated every aspect of a pagan culture, the living conditions and health of its people have improved. Even in ancient times God promised His people that they would have none of the diseases of the ungodly if they obeyed His commands concerning personal and corporate hygiene. Throughout the history of Western civilization, whenever these rules of cleanliness were heeded, people's lives improved. On the contrary, when the Gospel was hidden under a bushel, or when the salt was flavorless, terrible plagues came upon societies.

In America past, as the general population increasingly observed Biblical cleanliness, the health of our people improved and infant death rates dropped. Since medicine has become humanistic and anti-Christian, it has become anti-life. The result has been an absence of sound health, a lack of attention on the prevention of disease, and a drop in births (or shall we say, an increase in deaths as a result of infant murder/abortion). The revolt against authority in the sixties resulted in an increase of certain diseases and a general decline in sanitary living conditions. The wisdom of the past was turned upon its head, and dirt and filth were held in high esteem. Our society has not yet recovered from this leap backward toward death. It will be the Christian rebuilding of our private and public lives that will ensure our health and preserve our lives.

When teaching our children habits of cleanliness, we must keep in mind that this is also a fulfillment of God's command to love Him, love ourselves, and love our neighbors. When we care for our bodies with nourishment or good hygiene, we prevent disease and preserve life. We must love our families and neighbors enough not to bring sickness and disease on them.

Clean bodies and clothing are important to good health. Little babies should be bathed at least in part every day. The head, neck, hands, and diaper area should receive daily cleansing. Neglecting to clean this last area thoroughly can result in diaper rash or inflamed genitals.

Babies have a determined habit of putting hands and other objects into their mouths. As the hands are the primary carriers of sickness and disease, keep your child's hands clean. Continually work at training your baby or toddler to keep his hands out of his mouth. He should not be allowed to touch his genitals or bottom when being diapered—or at other times. All toddlers and little children tend to pick their noses. Teach your child that this is an unclean habit and help him learn to use a handkerchief or tissue. Toddlers think it is quite grown-up to carry their own hanky, which can be a real asset when they have colds. Young children often put their fingers in their ears, especially when their hands are unoccupied. Keep earwax removed and teach your child not to put anything in his ears.

Your child needs to understand early that hands carry dirt and germs that make us sick and that we get these germs by touching things that are dirty and have germs. Start the hand-washing habit at the crawling stage. The hand-washing rule is to wash before every meal (and later, before preparing food, drying dishes, setting the table), after every trip to the toilet, after eating, and after working or playing outdoors. Clean hands are not only important to personal hygiene and the health of society as a whole, but they are a courtesy to others. A child with clean hands will not dirty the walls and furniture of the houses he inhabits or visits. Parents show disrespect for their neighbors when they allow their children to handle things when their hands are dirty from playing outside or messy from eating.

When your children are small, they may

have many colds and bouts with flu—although they may have them less frequently if they are home educated children. Be considerate of others: do not take a sick child out in public, especially if there is fever present or lots of coughing, sneezing, and runny, colored mucus. Teach your toddler not to cough and sneeze on others, and to cover his mouth when he feels one coming.

Health habits also apply to clothing and other personal items. A little child should learn to change his underclothes daily. He should not wear outer clothing that is soiled by drool, food, or dirt. Bed clothes should be changed frequently. If your baby is put to bed clean, his bed linens will not become dirty so often. Newborn and infant cradles should have a large, soft cloth (diaper or flannel blanket) fitted across the top of the mattress. This catches mucus and spit-ups and is easy to change daily. Older children should be responsible for having clean bodies (and particularly clean feet) before going to bed.

Children who learn to be neat and clean show respect for their own bodies. Being clean also eliminates body and clothing odors that are offensive to others. It is not necessary to be wealthy, or to have a large selection of clothing, to maintain cleanliness. Everyone is capable of cleanliness, which is ultimately an act of love towards oneself and others.

Self-Restraint

The topic of toilet training has been hotly debated for many years. Dr. Spock's recommendations, from the late 1930s on, ranged from starting toilet training at twelve months to leaving it entirely up to the child. Unknowing parents thought his views were some important medical discovery but, unfortunately, as he later revealed, the ideas really just "came out of his head." [17]

Potty training is a very important aspect of training a child for maturity. For a child, learning to control or hold back elimination is a big step toward leaving his childish, selfish ways behind. It is a sad thing that many young mothers have been deceived by all sorts of theories of child psychologists. Horrible maladies are predicted for the child whose oppressive mother dares to teach him to use the toilet too early—from stuttering to incurable psychological problems later in life. In this instance, as with so many others we've discussed, when we reject the lessons from previous generations, we abandon common sense and the wisdom that underlies it.

When walks to the outhouse and chamber pots were the order of the day, children were potty trained at early ages. And have you ever wondered about all those bare-bottomed babies on the mothers' backs in the missionaries' pictures? I did, for years. One day I was bold enough to ask questions of a missionary friend. She said she had only once in her encounters with little ones been wet on, and that instance had occurred because the baby had become frightened. She made an important observation: the mothers seemed to know when their children needed to go and they took them to the appropriate place. Does it not seem strange that American children are not learning to use the toilet until three and four years—and even later?

Potty training can begin as soon as the baby can sit up well alone (around eight months). It begins with mother observing times of urination, or when bowel movements are passed—generally, after a meal. Setting the little one on the potty for a short time with an interesting book gives him something to occupy his attention. (Never leave the eight- to ten-month-old to sit alone, for he may fall.) This time can be used as an opportunity to read to the child or for mother to do her personal grooming in the bathroom as she watches over the child.

During this early teaching time, learn to catch the signs that the child is about to eliminate. The most common sign is when the toddler goes off in a corner to play quietly. This is also an indication he knows that what he is doing should not be done in his pants! Taking notice of this behavior, mother can say, "Bobby, it is time to go potty." If you think he might have to go, set him on, whether he thinks so or not. Eventually, you will catch him at just the right moment. He should be greatly praised and allowed to watch you flush it away. The belief that children should not see their bowel movements being disposed of because they will feel like a part of them is being destroyed is ridiculous—and is probably one of those Freudian ideas that just "popped into someone's head."

Children mature at different times, but this fact has become a great excuse for not training a child to gain control over part of his life. Most children who are trained early are out of diapers anywhere from twelve months on. Nighttime control takes longer and sometimes boys take longer than girls. Do not give up too soon: what takes several months of practice for one child may take many more for another. The secret is constant, scheduled practice. Another myth is that a child should never be spanked for wetting and soiling his pants. This is not consistent with good discipline. A child who stubbornly will not use the toilet, when he has spent months practicing control and recognizing the signs, needs correction. Children from ages two to five who constantly "forget" to take time to go, or purposely soil or wet their pants, should be corrected.

There are two infantile activities that, in our

opinion, indicate lack of discipline in a healthy young child: one is prolonged thumb sucking (or use of pacifiers) and the other is lack of toilet training. There is either permissiveness or harshness, a general lack of standards, or disunity between parents (one dotes, the other overreacts and punishes in anger). These weaknesses in child training create insecurity in the child, causing him to rebel by being unwilling to adopt more mature behavior. If you have a child of three years or older still clinging to these babyish actions, you might prayerfully consider whether your child training lacks a godly perspective. It is ungodly to baby a child and to hold him back from maturity.

Toilet training takes time and wisdom. What part of child training does not require these ingredients? Success is experienced as the child grows. To ignore this important part of mature conduct, because of the counsel of those with unscriptural philosophies of child training, is detrimental to godly character training.

Quietness

Quietness must be taught at an early age. Even the baby should be taught to be courteous, and not allowed to scream and bellow for all his desires and needs. Babies do make noise and we should not expect them to be silent all day long. However, they can be gradually taught to play quietly, not to speak and cry aloud, and to whisper for certain periods of time. This courtesy is important in the home as well as in public places. As the baby is learning the verbal "No" (with negative tone), start teaching quietness. Mother, spend time reading and praying for short periods during the day with your baby on your lap. When the baby begins to babble say, "No, shhh," and place your fingers over his lips. Practice this several times a day. An excellent opportunity to teach quietness is at thanksgiving prayers before meals. When meal thanks is said, gently clasp your baby's hands together. Gradually teach him not to speak and to shut his eyes. Your toddler may show stubbornness and attempt to not cooperate. He may wrench his hands away or make a loud protest and whine when you try to hush him. This is defiance to your command and cause for a spanking. Following the spanking and restoration, make him follow your original command. You may eat cold dinner more than once but you will have crossed a major threshold into obedience.

Church nurseries are a detriment to training little children. Let us face it, babies and children are put in nurseries because they are noisy and do not sit still. How will a child ever learn to be quiet if he is not made to be quiet and to practice it in public? Teach your babies to observe periods of quietness during the week. Train them to respond to your commands to be still and quiet, and they will be able to sit in the worship service with you on Sunday. The courtesy of quietness is also needed in many everyday situations, whether at the grocery store, Aunt Sally's house, or the doctor's office. A quiet child shows respect for other people.

One other application of this quietness rule applies during the spanking. A child may start to scream before the rod has hit even once. Do not allow your child to respond with loud anger and other over-dramatizations that show defiance of your authority. Susanna Wesley, mother of nineteen children, is well known for her rule to "cry softly" after chastisement.

Industry

God intends for man to be industrious. The dominion mandate requires man to be diligent in his work. Man's revolt against God's command in the Garden affected his ability and desire to work. Man fluctuates between laziness and worship of his work. Sloth (or idleness) seems to be our most common problem. Proverbs has plenty to say against the sluggard, and the Gospels and the Epistles also speak for laboring and being occupied in work.

In our day many people think childhood should be one uninterrupted, gleeful vacation. Many children occupy most of their time throughout childhood with self-centered play. As previously noted, the Bible speaks of man's life as being blessed in work and in rest. Play, idleness, riotous living, and pursuit of pleasure are all treated negatively, and man is commanded not to seek fulfillment or spend his energies seeking leisure. This generation's parents experience a great deal of guilt and fear about requiring their children to work.

Today's adults hold two unbiblical beliefs. The first is that work is a curse and leisure is a blessing. Life's goal, therefore, has become complete leisure—no responsibility and no productivity. The second belief is that childhood must be a time of fun because work is unpleasant and robs childhood of its joyous freedom from responsibility. Of course, these beliefs are based on faulty assumptions about God, His creation of man, and His commands to him.

True Christian training focuses on preparing the child for adult work, thoroughly equipping him for God's purposes. Ask God to renew your mind so that you will find joy in productive work. If mother and father have an ungodly view toward their God-given responsibilities, they can expect their child to be an accomplished "escape artist" also.

The child's foolishness is what drives him to seek more and more freedom from responsibility or to pursue constant play. It is your responsibility to train him early to obey God's mandate to work. Do not wait to teach industry until you have a youthful sluggard. Your toddler can learn to be a helper and can find great pride in being one. Require him to help keep the house clean by having him put away his own toys. A young child should not be allowed to take all his toys out and leave them lying about when he goes on to another activity. A good rule is that only toys being played with may be out and that those must be returned before others may be taken out. The eighteen- to twenty-four-month-old child can learn to do the dishes by standing on a chair and rinsing them under your supervision. Other simple tasks, such as emptying waste baskets, putting away clutter, shaking throw rugs, and dusting, can be taught to a very young child.

Proper attitudes toward work can be taught early, eliminating problems with murmuring and laziness later. Your child should know he is pleasing God when he does the tasks you have assigned him. He must be a God-pleaser first. Let him experience the joy of working with you or an older brother or sister. He will be encouraged because of the companionship, but he will also need your watchful eye so that he will do his job well and finish it. Eventually require him to do his regular tasks unsupervised. He must learn to be a good steward when his master is absent, making good use of his time and doing the job according to directions.

A dawdler must be taught that wasting time is not pleasing to the Lord and breaks His command not to steal. (Wasting time is stealing from others.) Set reasonable time limits for simple tasks. Many times words do not cure the dawdler, but the rod does. Forgetfulness is a very serious trait that needs to be controlled. The toddler should continue from one-step instructions to two-step, then three. (For example, "Please put these towels in the bathroom drawer . . . and bring me the hair brush . . . and your pink barrettes . . . and one ponytail band.") Help the child develop his ability to remember by giving instructions for a task that is to be accomplished sometime in the future. (For example, "When you finish lunch, please go up and empty the waste baskets.") Never allow your child to whine or pout about work he is asked to do. It is defiance of your authority when your child protests, "I can't . . ."; "I don't want to . . ."; "Do I have to right now?"; "In a minute . . ." Nip this disobedience at the toddler stage with a spanking.

The chore chart is an efficient method for delegating household duties and other responsibilities. Each child is given a list of chores to complete on various days of the week. The chore chart helps the children learn about planning (setting a goal to make good use of time), keeps them organized (they never wonder what to do), and shows them how productive they have been. They must also understand that these are not the only tasks they will be asked to do, so that there will be no murmuring about extra work.

Children who are constantly bored ("Mom, there's nothing to do!"), discontented ("I don't have anything/anyone to play with!"), and looking for entertainment ("Can't I go to the movies?", or, "Can't I go to John's house?") are children who have had too much leisure. If your children have become sluggards, ask God to forgive your sin and to show you how and why you trained them this way. When you repent, tell your children how you have disobeyed God and that in obedience to God, and for their own good, things will be different. Teach your children to view their home as the center of their work and rest. They must expect to contribute to the family economy, giving loving service to parents, brothers, and sisters. We must never accept guilt from the Accuser, Satan, for giving our children work, because work is the very thing God called man to do.

Honesty

Training a young child to be honest in his words and actions is very challenging. Dishonesty or guile is one of the great heart diseases of man.

The nature of dishonesty is that it is often done in secret. Like Adam and Eve, none of us likes to admit, "I did it." Children must learn to confess their wrongdoing. This prepares them to confess their sin to God. When a child initiates confessing his sin, he should be forgiven. Of course, he should be required to make the proper restitution for his error.

BE CERTAIN to teach him about God's absolute and certain forgiveness when he repents.

For instance, if a child accidentally breaks or damages another child's toy while playing, and he admits to the damage without being asked, the rod is not necessary, but repairing or replacing the toy is required. However, when a parent knows that a child has committed sin and then confronts the child and he repeatedly denies or tries to justify himself, he should be chastised for the sin and also for lying. If a child is taught God's Word from infancy, he will know lying is a sin. Be certain to teach him about God's absolute and certain forgiveness when he repents. Never assume he is lying if there is not sufficient proof. Sometimes circumstances can be very complicated, especially if other children are involved, and it is hard to determine just who did what. If you suspect he is lying, ask God to reveal it to you clearly so that you can deal with it. He will.

A child who denies wrongdoing or makes up stories to justify his sin is probably dishonest in other ways. When simple questions are directed to him, he may seem to evade the truth. A prevaricator cannot easily answer the question, "What are you doing?" even though he is innocent. He may feel compelled to tell pompous stories about his wonderful accomplishments or be the family clown. This tendency to exaggerate may come from pride or trying to compete with another family member.

SECULAR PSYCHOLOGISTS say that babies who are allowed to explore, free from almost all restraint, are more intelligent and self-confident. This is simply not true.

A child may also be deceitful and sneaky in his actions. He may secretly pocket Dad's loose change or sneak cookies. The toddler must learn that "no" means "no," even when father and mother are not looking. If you are faithful to set boundaries and standards and enforce them, then, when he is between two and three years old, your child should be able to be trusted for short periods when he is out of your sight. Most babies who learn to not touch or explore everything they see will be more trustworthy as they mature. Secular psychologists say that babies who are allowed to explore, free from almost all restraint, are more intelligent and self-confident. This is simply not true. It is the child who learns self-government or control through consistent, loving training who becomes wise (Proverbs 15:31–33).

Lies are in the infant's heart from the start and we should not be shocked when we see dishonesty manifested early. Do endeavor to live honestly yourself and to teach your child God's hatred for lying lips and deceitful hearts. Take action against lying as you would other acts of disobedience.

Chapter 5

THE FATHER'S DUTY TO ESTABLISH LOVING DISCIPLINE

*F*OR HE ESTABLISHED *a testimony in Jacob, and appointed a law in Israel, which He commanded our fathers, that they should make them known to their children; that the generation to come might know them, the children who would be born, that they may arise and declare them to their children, that they may set their hope in God, and not forget the works of God, but keep His commandments; and may not be like their fathers, a stubborn and rebellious generation, a generation that did not set its heart aright, and whose spirit was not faithful to God. (Psalm 78:5–8)*

Throughout Scripture, the primary responsibility for bringing up obedient, well-mannered children rests on the father. In fact, it is such a strong requirement that a man should not be considered for, let alone be allowed to hold, a leadership position in the church if his children are uncontrollable.

The sooner the father recognizes his responsibility with regard to bringing up his children, the easier and more effective his job will be. There will be greater joy within the family and that joy will affect other areas of life as well.

The purpose of discipline is to keep children from a destructive course and to build strong Christian character. In days of distress this will enable them to walk in faith (Psalm 94:12,13). We are not to just bring up children that are merely "okay," but children that are truly godly in their thoughts and actions.

A FATHER must be diligent in enforcing and maintaining standards for obedience.

A father who is lax in personal and active nurturing is self-centered, which is often manifested by a "don't bother me I'm busy" attitude, and is not acting in love. In contrast, there are three ways in which a father can personally and actively direct the character training of his children. First, he must be diligent in enforcing and maintaining standards for obedience. As the head of the home, God has given him the duty to set the standards for conduct. These standards are clearly stated in Scripture, as noted throughout this book. It seems that many fathers today are not being taught their responsibility to search the Scripture, nor to use this standard in governing their homes.

Secondly, loving nurture is carried out by the father who gives attention to family life. He does this by being watchful over his children's behavior at all times (Psalm 32:8). However, many times the father—when his wife is present—leaves the disciplining to her, or even others, whether at home or in public. Some call this delegating—God calls it neglect. Watching over his children's conduct should be the focus of a father's attention, even though he is carrying on a conversation with others or engrossed in a project. It is true that this is a shared responsibility, but the father is held accountable for the behavior of his household.

Next, the father should consider his wife's assessment of his children's needs. She observes the children all day and often recognizes existing or potential problems with attitude and behavior that need correction. Also, she will see unfolding skills and talents that need to be encouraged and developed.

One of the most important ways a father nurtures his family is through prayer, and it is important for him to realize that to have his prayers heard by God he must first love his wife.

1 Peter 3:7 commands, "Likewise you husbands, dwell with them with understanding, giving honor to the wife, as to the weaker vessel, and as being heirs together of the grace of life, that your prayers may not be hindered." Colossians 3:19 states, "Husbands, love your wives . . ." Again, in Ephesians 5:25, "Husbands, love your wives, just as Christ loved the church and gave Himself for it." Notice that the husband's duty is to love his wife, understand her needs, and meet them. By doing so he creates an atmosphere of love in the entire home. In this loving atmosphere, he can pray for his children's salvation, attitudes, Christian conduct, their future vocations, and marriages.

Finally, loving nurture is carried out by the father who is an example to his children in work and rest. He does this by teaching them how to work, directing Lord's Day rest and worship, enjoying recreation with them, and teaching them a craft or hobby.

As has been previously established, discipline not only encompasses nurture, the training of character, but also admonition, or counsel to the intellect. In other words, admonition is the verbal instruction that you are to give to your family. In our modern culture, this important duty of the father is probably one of the most neglected.

Scriptural admonition is accomplished in

two ways. First, conducting family worship should be a routine part of the family schedule. The children should sense the father's respect for the Word of God by hearing him read it often. The Proverbs are especially important for training in Christian conduct—from infancy through adulthood. The singing of psalms and doctrinally sound, God-honoring hymns should also be included in family worship.

T HE CHILDREN **should sense the father's respect for the Word of God by hearing him read it often.**

Secondly, reading and studying the Scriptures and worthwhile books—by the parents as well as by the children—are important means for admonishing children character qualities that can be taught through the enjoyment of Christian biographies, church history, and other historical biographies. With regard to family study, Romans 12:2 states, "And be not conformed to this world, but be transformed by the renewing of your mind, that you may prove what is that good and acceptable and perfect will of God."

A renewed mind comes through the knowledge of correctly interpreted Scripture. Young children and youth need to be taught Bible study methods, critical thinking skills, and the doctrines of our faith. This continual and purposeful admonition will enable them to become strong in their beliefs and in no danger of being drawn away into heresy.

Before I explain the methods I have practiced in our home, I want to assure other fathers that I am human; because I am imperfect, I do not always act consistently with my goals and ideals. However, I do know that the Lord has set the pattern for me and by His grace I am trying to conform my life to it.

The most important habit I have been striving to establish is the daily teaching of our children. Each day I read Scripture and pray with them. This gives them a pattern to imitate in their own lives—both now and later. A few days a week, I read about and discuss pertinent topics that come to our attention. This is an excellent opportunity to find out how much the children understand about important issues of life and where they need further teaching. At other times, I may read aloud Christian and historical biographies.

Some key factors have enabled us to accomplish these goals for our family. One factor is that we do not have a time-robbing TV in our home. This does not mean that we never watch TV, because we do occasionally. It does mean that very little of our family life is spent in front of a television. A second important part of our way of life is that our children seldom take part in strictly youth-oriented activities, such as Sunday school, youth groups, or clubs. Instead, our family participates primarily in adult family-oriented gatherings and meetings. Also, regarding "peer socialization," we have encouraged them to have a few well-chosen, Christian friends, and most of their contact with them has been in family settings—birthday parties, church family activities, Bible studies, holiday gatherings, out-of-town visiting, and family meals that include guests.

O**NE OF the most important ways a father nurtures his family is through prayer.**

As a final word of encouragement, you can be assured that I have kept everything very simple and have varied the subjects, materials, and methods I have used throughout the years. This was done for two reasons: the demands of my work schedule and the fact that my wife and I do not consider ourselves to be intellectuals. Truthfully, neither one of us was ever considered a good student or voted "most likely to succeed" during our school years. It has been in commit-

ting ourselves to home schooling that we have
seen the Lord making us more knowledgeable
about, and faithful to, our Christian calling.

In Psalm 128, promises are given to the
father who governs his family according to
God's commands:

"Blessed is every one who fears the Lord,
who walks in His ways. When you eat the labor
of your hands, you shall be happy, and it shall be
well with you. Your wife shall be like a fruitful
vine in the very heart of your house; your children like olive plants all around your table.
Behold, thus shall the man be blessed who fears
the Lord. The Lord bless you out of Zion, and
may you see the good of Jerusalem all the days of
your life. Yes, may you see your children's children. Peace be upon Israel!" [18]

Chapter 6

SUSANNA WESLEY: THE LEGACY OF A VIRTUOUS MOTHER

T HEREFORE I DESIRE *that the younger women marry, bear children, manage the house, give no opportunity to the adversary to speak reproachfully. (1 Timothy 5:14) [A]dmonish the young women to love their husbands, love their children, to be discreet, chaste, home-makers, good, obedient to their own husbands, that the word of God may not be blasphemed. (Titus 2:4,5)*

History has bequeathed us an honorable mother whose example is worthy of emulation. That mother was Susanna Wesley. She knew what it meant to love her children and train them up for the Lord. She also paid the price. In later years she wrote to a son:

"No one can, without renouncing the world, in the most literal sense, observe my method; and there are few, if any, that would entirely devote above twenty years of the prime of life in hopes to save the souls of their children, which they think may be saved without so much ado . . ." [19]

Susanna was committed to her marriage vows and seriously dedicated her life to training the children God had entrusted to the Wesley union. Her life was complicated by twenty years of pregnancies and childbearing, poverty, ungodly neighbors, and having a husband away on extended trips.

In our day, as in Susanna's, many mothers do not think it is necessary to "renounce the world" in order to bring children to maturity. Today's mother is constantly urged and tempted to find fulfillment in empty pursuits outside the home. There is constant encouragement to enroll children in endless outside activities to supposedly give Mother the freedom to discover herself and to develop her own personal goals.

For Susanna and other godly mothers, renouncing the world means forsaking selfish desires and seeking God's perfect purpose for women. We must remember that forsaking our selfish desires is an age-old battle that has never been an easy one, and it always requires spiritual weapons of war. (2 Corinthians 10:3–5; Ephesians 6:10–18)

Susanna's "method" of child rearing is inspiring and instructive. Her dedication to her calling and her determination to maintain an ordered household—under the most impossible circumstances—was often manifested in very creative ways. With so many children needing her attention, it is easy to imagine the difficulty she experienced in finding time to pray. Her creative solution was to teach her children to not disturb her at prayer whenever she placed her apron over her head. She used no excuses—even very valid ones—such as too many children and their interruptions, or too much work, to neglect her habits of private worship.

Today's mother is constantly urged and tempted to find fulfillment in empty pursuits outside the home . . . we must remember that forsaking our selfish desires is an age-old battle.

At the heart of Susanna's "method" is the commitment to "save the souls" of our children, a commitment that requires a mother's diligent, loving attention to the details of life. Many modern mothers lack the motivation to manage their homes in such a way that children will grow to be mature through the practice of good habits. Christian homes require careful and consistent management by mothers who understand the impact that orderly and productive living can have on their children's souls.

Like Susanna Wesley, many virtuous mothers believe strongly in God and His commands and live lives contrary to the flow of our times. They know that the true joy during this life, and at its end, is to see their children living for the Lord. These are women worthy of honor because they take great pains and make many sacrifices to make certain that their children are brought up in God's way.

Appendix A

Warning Signs

*A*S PARENTS, *we must responsibly act with the authority that has been given to us. We are accountable to God for the proper discipline of our children.*

These signs indicate my child is not learning good character traits. They signal that I am losing control or not in authority in my home:

1. My child whines, cries, and pouts when I say "no" to him.

2. I find myself reluctant to ask my child to help with any tasks because of his negative reaction and inability to complete a job. He usually responds to my requests by whining or answers, "I can't..." or "I don't want to..."

3.   There is an excessive amount of noise and confusion in my house: screaming, bickering, crying, hitting, rough behavior with furniture or toys, etc.

4.   I am unable to leave food snacks or anything of personal value within my child's reach.

5.   I am unable to leave my child (aged three or above) out of my sight or unattended in another room for any period of time without being worried about what he is up to.

6.   I am embarrassed or afraid to take my child to other homes because he is so active (boisterous, silly, fidgety; he knocks things over and touches everything).

7.   My child is unable to sit quietly for any length of time in a place I specify.

8.   Going shopping is a fiasco because my children run through the clothes racks, or touch everything in the store, or run away from me.

9.   My child has a "smart mouth" (yells, uses abusive language, swears at me) or hits me.

10. My child throws tantrums, refuses to eat or do what he is asked to do.

11. My child takes things without asking and rummages through our drawers and cupboards.

12. My child does not come when called or respond to my voice from another room.

13. When I ask my child to do something I always have to explain "why" first.

14. Many of my child's toys are broken and he rarely puts any away—outdoors or indoors.

15. My child avoids doing what I ask by using flattering words, changing the subject, or doing some other good deed instead.

16. My child gets my attention with loud, disrespectful demands, e.g.,"Hey, Mom! Get the ___ for me!" or "I want ___ !" or "Mom, come here!"

17. I find myself saying, "I can't do that because Suzy won't let me" or "I can't get Johnny to do that..."

18. When I spank my child he pouts, responds in anger, screams, throws himself on the floors, slams doors, prolongs his crying, coughs, or gags (attempts to vomit).

19. As I talk on the phone or chat with others, my child constantly interrupts or acts naughty, demanding my attention.

20. My child is constantly bored, discontent, and looking for entertainment; wanting to play, he grumbles at his work.

21. I am ready to pull my hair out. My child drives me crazy. I am so worn out all the time that I can hardly wait to get a break from him at every opportunity.

A note to parents: How sharp is your Scripture memory? Can you think of a verse dealing with each of the above? These are examples of poor character qualities that the Bible—especially Proverbs—addresses.

Appendix B

THE DISCIPLINED CHILD

"HE WHO BEGETS A WISE CHILD
WILL DELIGHT IN HIM."

—Proverbs 23:24b

*The chart on the overleaf corresponds to
the discussion of a wise child in chapter two.*

❧ *Accepts discipline. Prov. 13:1a "A wise son heeds his father's instruction. (Hebrew word, chastening)" Prov. 15:32; Eph. 6:1*

❧ *Obeys all commands. Col. 3:20 "Children, obey your parents in all things." Gen. 28:7; 47:31; Prov. 23:22*

❧ *Replaces natural foolishness and youthful lusts with wisdom and good behavior. 1 Pet. 1:14 "As obedient children, not conforming yourselves to the former lusts, as in your ignorance." Prov. 23:15; Tit. 2:6; 1 Tim. 4:12; 2 Tim. 2:22,23; Eccl. 11:9,10*

❧ *Is mindful of his Creator. Eccl. 12:1 "Remember now your Creator in the days of your youth."*

❧ *Learns to know and value the Word. 2 Tim. 3:15 "From childhood you have known the Holy Scriptures."*

❧ *Honors, loves, and respects parents and authority. Lev. 19:3,32 "Every one of you shall revere his mother and his father...You shall rise before the gray headed, and honor the presence of an old man..." Gen. 45:11; Ex. 20:12; Eph. 6:2*

BENEFITS OF A DISCIPLINED CHARACTER

❧ *The Lord is with him. 1 Sam. 3:19*
Gains understanding or self-esteem.
Prov. 15:32b

❧ *Pleases God. Col. 3:20b*

❧ *Brings his parents joy and gladness.*
Prov. 10:1; 27:11; 23:15, 16, 24; 29:17b.
Respected as an example by others.
1 Tim. 4:12

❧ *Serves God with the best days of his life.*
Eccl. 12:1

❧ *By God's choosing, a wise child comes to*
understand and receive salvation through
faith in Christ Jesus. 2 Tim 3:15

❧ *Successful, long life. Eph. 6:3; Deut. 5:16*

See Proverbs for many more
characteristics of a wise child...

Appendix C

THE UNDISCIPLINED CHILD

"HE WHO BEGETS A FOOL DOES SO
TO HIS SORROW, AND THE FATHER OF
A FOOL HAS NO JOY."

—Proverbs 17:21

▼ *Does not listen to reproof; is stubborn and rebellious. Prov. 13:1b "A scoffer does not listen to rebuke." Deut 21:18*

▼ *Disobeys and rejects discipline. Prov. 15:32 "He who disdains instruction (Hebrew word, chastening) despises his own soul." 15:5; Deut 21:18; Rom. 1:30; 2 Tim. 3:2*

▼ *Speaks with disrespect and swears at parents. Prov. 20:20 "...curses his father or his mother." Prov. 30:11, 17; Mk. 7:10*

▼ *Slanders his parents. Prov. 19:26*

▼ *Steals from and takes advantage of his parents. Prov. 28:24 "...robs his father or his mother, and says 'It is no transgression.'" Deut. 21:20b*

▼ *May fatally strike parents or betray them. Ex. 21:15 "...he who strikes his father or his mother..." Mk. 13:12; Mk. 7:10; Prov. 20:20*

▼ *Arrogantly rejects authority and despises elders. Isa. 3:5; "The people will be oppressed, every one by another...The child will be insolent toward the elder..." Prov. 23:22*

▼ *Is foolish and lacks understanding. Prov. 10:1; 22:15; 7:7 "...And [I] saw among the simple, I perceived among the youths, a young man devoid of understanding."*

CONSEQUENCES OF BAD CHARACTER

▼ *His life ends in ruin. Prov. 5:11–14. He inherits punishment for sins of his youth. Job 13:26. Parents denounce and relinquish responsibility to provide for and protect him. Deut 21:19*

▼ *He hates himself. Prov. 15:32a. He is rejected by God (reprobate). Rom. 1:28*

▼ *He loses prosperity. Prov. 20:20b. He dies in shame. Prov. 30:17; Lev. 20:9*

▼ *He is a shame and disgrace to his parents. Prov. 19:26*

▼ *He is considered an equal with criminals. Prov. 28:24*

▼ *He is condemned to death. Ex. 21:15; Lev. 20:9*

▼ *Social unrest, anarchy, and youth in revolt. Isa. 3:4,5, 12–26*

▼ *His life is destroyed; he brings shame, grief, and disgrace to his parents. Prov. 19:13a, 26b; 17:25*

REFERENCES

DeGraaf, S.G. *Promise and Deliverance.* Vol. 1. Ontario: Paideia Press, 1977. (Available through the Westminster Discount Book Service, P.O. Box 125H, Scarsdale, NY, 10583, (914) 472-2237).

Fabrizio, Al and Pat. *Under Loving Command.* Palo Alto: Sheva Press, 1969. (Available from Sheva Press, P.O. Box 183, Palo Alto, CA., 94302).

Fugate, Richard. *What the Bible Says About Child Training.* Tempe, AZ: Aletheia Publishers, Inc., 1980.

Harmon, Rebecca L. *Susanna, Mother of the Wesleys.* Nashville: Abingdon Press, 1968.

Holzmann, John. *Dating with Integrity: Honoring Christ in your Relationships with the Opposite Sex.* Brentwood, TN: Wolgemuth & Hyatt Publishers, Inc., 1990.

Ray, Bruce. *Withhold Not Correction.* Nutley, NJ: Presbyterian and Reformed Publishing Co., 1978.

Schlect, Christopher. *Critique of Modern Youth Ministry.* Moscow, ID: Canon Press, 1995.

ENDNOTES

1. Richard Fugate, *What the Bible Says About Child Training* (Tempe, AZ: Aletheia Publishers, Inc., 1980),143.

   The author states, "Remember, God's Word commands that children are to obey their parents. It is the child who chooses to break God's law. The parents are merely enforcing God's law when they must chastise a rebellious child."

2. Howard Ahmanson, [title unknown], Chalcedon Report 197 (January 1982).

3. R. J. Rushdoony, *The Philosophy of the Christian Curriculum* (Vallecito, CA: Ross House Books, 1981), 122.

4. Christopher Schlect, *Critique of Modern Youth Ministry* (Moscow, ID: Canon Press, 1995), 11.

   This booklet is recommended for parents and leaders that are concerned about their church youth groups and desire to make some Biblical changes. Order from: Canon Press, 116 West "C" Street, Moscow, ID 83843. Phone number is (208) 882-1456.

5. Ibid., 10.

6. S. G. DeGraaf, *Promise and Deliverance, vol. 1* (St. Catherines, Ontario, Canada: Paideia Press, 1977), 19,20.

7. R. J. Rushdoony, The Institutes of Biblical Law (Phillipsburg, NJ: Presbyterian and Reformed Publishing Company, 1973), 198.

8. Ibid., 166. The author states, "A revolutionary age breaks with the past and turns on parents with animosity and venom: it disinherits itself."

9. Lyn Z. Bloom, *Doctor Spock* (New York: Bobbs Merrill Co., Inc., 1972), 132.

10. Paul Copperman, *The Literacy Hoax* (New York: William Morrow and Co., 1978), 145.

    The author states that child rearing advice of the forties and fifties created egocentric, demanding, manipulative children who grew up with an unrealistic sense of ego power and self-importance during the sixties to seventies, developing a contempt and hostility for adults. [These "children" are now parents that have no concept of the Biblical meaning of authority.]

11. C.D. Ginsberg, "Leviticus," *Ellicott's Commentary on the Whole Bible* (Grand Rapids, MI: Zondervan) 1:421f., quoted in Rushdoony, Institutes, 170.

12. Bruce Ray, *Withhold Not Correction* (Nutley, NJ: Presbyterian and Reformed Publishing Co., 1978), 148.

    The author states that "Our motive for discipline is to bring our children into a subordinate relationship to the authority of the living God and not just ourselves." We are in full agreement but wish to add that you are God's appointed authority over your child and that the offense is to you as well. You are His representative.

13. Otto J. Scott, [title unknown], Chaldecon Report 218, (September 1983).

14. Al and Pat Fabrizio, *Under Loving Command* (Palo Alto, CA: Sheva Press, 1969).

   In our opinion, this pamphlet is the clearest and most Biblical teaching on the use of the rod that is available.

15. Bloom, *Doctor Spock*, 84, 127, 135.

   Spock broke totally with the Christian view of God and man and religiously applied the theories of Freud (animal-man driven by bodily functions and sexual energy) and Dewey (permissiveness; learning by experience and feeling) to child training. Bloom defends Spock's early teaching by saying, "Those who condemn Dr. Spock's 'permissiveness' are reacting essentially to the first edition of Baby and Child Care [1946] WHICH WAS TRYING TO HELP PARENTS DEAL WITH RIGID AND ARBITRARY DOCTRINES THAT NO LONGER EXIST... *[emphasis ours]," p. 140.*

16. John Holzmann, *Dating with Integrity: Honoring Christ in your Relationships with the Opposite Sex* (Brentwood, TN: Wolgemuth & Hyatt Publishers, Inc., 1990).

   Holzmann builds a strong case for getting back to Biblical youthful relationships and courtship.

17. Bloom, Doctor Spock, 102.

18. This Psalm can be found in the *Psalter,* or in the *Trinity Hymnal,* "Blest the Man Who Fears Jehovah," 1961 edition, p. 626.

19. Rebecca L. Harmon, Susanna, Mother of the Wesleys, (Nashville: Abingdon Press, 1968), 57

_____

_____

_____

_____

_____

_____

_____

_____

_____

_____

_____

_____

_____

THE ELSIE BOOKS
THE ORIGINAL SERIES BY MARTHA FINLEY

Spanning over 38 years, Martha Finley penned the adventures of Elsie Dinsmore, often using members of her own family for characterization. Truth, faith, religion, morality, and humanity are all underlying virtues in this extraordinary series of children's fiction.

As Miss Finley's stories evolve, Elsie Dinsmore is faced with a myriad of trials and tribulations. Elsie's devout faith and clear knowledge of Scripture enable her to persevere through each troublesome circumstance. As Elsie matures into a godly woman, so her unique family grows, adding to the lovable — and sometimes not so likeable — cast of Miss Finley's interesting characters.

In 1868, the New York firm of Dodd Mead released the first "Elsie" book, *Elsie Dinsmore*. Quickly becoming a bestseller for the publisher, it launched the successful series, *The Elsie Books*. Martha Finley became one of the most renowned children's writers of her time, with book sales second only to Louisa May Alcott.

Hibbard Publications is honored to continue this heartwarming series, bringing back values and faith that are jeopardized in today's society. We hope you enjoy *The Elsie Books*.

Available from Your Local Bookstore.
Available to the Trade through Ingram/Spring Arbor,
Appalachian, Baker & Taylor, or Riverside World

 **HIBBARD PUBLICATIONS** is pleased to publish books that preserve family values. Check your local bookstore for these fine titles.

- *The Elsie Books* by Elsie Dinsmore
  28 Volumes
- *History Alive Through Music Book & Tape Series*
  by Diana Waring, et. al.
  Westward Ho! The Heart of the Old West
  Musical Memories of Laura Ingalls Wilder
  America 1750–1890: Heart of a New Land
- *Wise Words: Family Stories that Bring Proverbs to Life*
  by Peter Leithart
- *You're Going To Do What? Helping You Understand the*
  Homeschool Decision by Laurajean Downs
- *Dinner's in the Freezer* by Jill Bond
  Textbook Size
  Trade Size
- *Writing to God's Glory: A Comprehensive Creative*
  Writing Course from Crayon to Quill by Jill Bond

Also carried by Hibbard Publications:
- *Miserly Moms: Living on One Income in a Two*
  Income Economy by Jonni McCoy
- *Frugal Families: Making the Most Out Of Your Hard*
  Earned Money by Jonni McCoy

Available to the Trade through Ingram / Spring Arbor,
Appalachian, Baker & Taylor, or Riverside World.